Guide to
Presentations

Prentice Hall "Guide To"
Series in Business Communication

Guide to
Presentations

Third Edition

Lynn Russell
Professional Development Company

Mary Munter
Tuck School of Business Dartmouth College

Prentice Hall

Boston   Columbus   Indianapolis   New York   San Francisco   Upper Saddle River   Amsterdam
Cape Town   Dubai   London   Madrid   Milan   Munich   Paris   Montreal   Toronto   Delhi
Mexico City   Sao Paulo   Sydney   Hong Kong   Seoul   Singapore   Taipei   Tokyo

Editorial Director: Sally Yagan
Editor in Chief: Eric Svendsen
Acquisitions Editor: James Heine
Product Development Manager:
 Ashley Santora
Director of Marketing: Patrice Lumumba Jones
Marketing Manager: Nikki Jones
Marketing Assistant: Ian Gold
Senior Managing Editor: Judy Leale
Project Manager: Debbie Ryan
Operations Specialist: Clara Bartunek
Creative Director: Jayne Conte
Cover Designer: Bruce Kenselaar

Manager, Visual Research: Beth Brenzel
Manager, Rights and Permissions:
 Shannon Barbe
Manager, Cover Visual Research
 & Permissions: Karen Sanatar
Cover Image: Getty Images, Inc.
Full-Service Project Management:
 Aparna Yellai, PreMediaGlobal
Composition: PreMediaGlobal
Printer/Binder: Edwards Brothers, Inc.
Cover Printer: Lehigh-Phoenix
 Color/Hagerstown
Text Font: 10.5/12 Times

Table of Contents

PART I
PRESENTATION
STRATEGY

PART II
PRESENTATION
IMPLEMENTATION

CHAPTER 4

CHAPTER 5

CHAPTER 6

Introduction

CHANGES TO NEW EDITION

Although we have incorporated minor revisions on many pages, by far the most important change is the focus on PowerPoint visuals in Chapter 5. Rather than discuss all types of visual aids, the chapter now addresses only PowerPoint visuals—both standard PowerPoint slides and presentation decks. The chapter walks you through the process of creating these visuals and offers ideas on how to work around some of the PowerPoint defaults that can lead to needlessly complex slides or pages.

In addition to the major changes in Chapter 5, you will also find minor ones in Chapter 1 (Audience Analysis) and Chapter 4 (Structure).

Changes in Chapter 1: Audience Analysis

- *Expanded "What will persuade them?" section:* We moved the information about decision makers and other influential audience members from the first question—"Who are they?"—to the final question about persuasion. Now our ABCs of persuasion include four headings: (1) assess various appeals; (2) build support with benefit statements; (3) consider your credibility; and (4) determine how to reach the decision makers.

- *Included pros and cons of various appeals:* Rather than just list persuasive techniques, we show the strengths and weaknesses of various appeals, such as quantitative appeals, benchmarking, and the other appeals mentioned in the previous editions. We encourage you to base their use on the interests and tendencies of the audience.

- *Differentiated general benefit statements from targeted ones:* The table that showed how to create benefit statements has been expanded into two tables. The first table shows the steps involved in developing a general statement that will tell the audience what's in it for them, while the second one shows how to target a benefit statement to the interests of an influential audience member.

Changes in Chapter 4: Structure

- *Added details about ordering content:*   In addition to listing common ordering techniques for persuasive presentations, we offer more extensive examples about how to organize presentations based on recommendations and benefits.

- *Clarified active listening paraphrasing versus Q&A paraphrasing:* We define standard paraphrasing and then compare it to the type used when taking questions during a presentation.

Changes in Chapter 5: Design PowerPoint Visuals

- *Added a table to compare slides and deck pages:*   We summarize the basic differences between slides and presentation decks to help you decide which format would best suit your presentation.

- *Included ideas about how to keep attention focused on you:*   We encourage you to connect with your audience by finding times to take visual aid breaks—moments when the audience's attention goes back to the presenter.

- *Explained how to set up a PowerPoint Slide Master:*   We guide you step-by-step through the process of choosing colors and setting up the Slide Master. We also explain why and how the Slide Master needs to be adjusted for deck pages since it was created for slides.

- *Suggested how to overcome flaws with company-provided templates:* We offer ideas about how to deal with company templates that have color issues, formatting flaws, and logos or other designs that take up too much of the slide or page.

- *Added information about SmartArt:*   PowerPoint's diagram maker, known as SmartArt, can tempt people to make diagrams that don't reinforce the right message. Therefore, we explain how to overcome some SmartArt challenges.

- *Expanded material about photographs:*   Too many people violate copyright laws by pasting photos from the web into their slide shows and presentation decks. Therefore, we include a list of where to find free and inexpensive photos that are legal to use and suggest how to choose and insert images.

- *Summarized "chartjunk" information:*   To eliminate the clutter that accompanies charts made in Excel and PowerPoint, we added a table that explains how to improve them.

HOW THIS BOOK CAN HELP YOU

When you are working on a presentation and have specific questions, refer to a page or section of this book for help. For example:

- If you are speaking to a new group of colleagues and wonder how you can come across as credible without seeming to brag, look at pages 20 and 21.
- If you have an important message that needs to stand out and want to know how to make it memorable, skim the first part of Chapter 3.
- If you are worried that someone is going to ask a question you can't answer, read the section on question and answer sessions, which starts on page 67.
- If you are making a presentation deck, but are more used to making PowerPoint slides, compare their differences with the table on page 78.
- If, like many other people, you feel nervous about presenting, check the tips for managing speech anxiety, which begin on page 136.

On the other hand, maybe you aren't working on a specific talk, but want general guidelines on how to become a better presenter. If so, read through the entire book. By doing so, you will know all the steps involved in preparing and delivering an effective presentation and have an easy-to-skim reference available when it's time to prepare and present your next talk.

WHY THIS BOOK WAS WRITTEN

Between the two of us, we've taught at many colleges and universities, including Stanford, Dartmouth, and Columbia. We've assisted business executives working in an array of industries and other leaders, ranging from directors of community groups to government officials on the other side of the globe. Our students and clients often say they want a resource that is both professional and readable. We have done our best to write a guide that matches those interests by using examples based on real presentations, relying on plain language, and including headings that are easy to skim.

HOW THIS BOOK IS ORGANIZED

The book is divided into two sections: strategy and implementation.

Part I: Presentation Strategy (Chapters 1–3)

Successful presentations are based on effective strategy. Effective strategy, in turn, is based on three strategic variables: audience, intent, and message. Together, they form what we refer to as "AIM" strategy.

- *Chapter 1: Analyze the Audience.* This chapter explains how to answer the questions: (1) Who are they? (2) What do they know and expect? (3) What do they feel? and (4) What will persuade them?

- *Chapter 2: Identify Your Intent.* This chapter recommends that you (1) consider your general purpose, (2) write a presentation objective, and (3) use this objective to focus as you prepare and present.

- *Chapter 3: Make the Most of the Message.* This chapter explains how to make your message memorable and why you need to confirm that a presentation is the best way to deliver your message.

Part II: Presentation Implementation (Chapters 4–6)

Part two explains how to apply AIM strategy to three implementation components: structure, visuals, and nonverbal delivery.

- *Chapter 4: Structure the Content.* This chapter takes you through the process of structuring your presentation: (1) collecting, focusing, and ordering information; (2) deciding what to say in the opening, body, and closing of your talk; and (3) preparing for the audience's questions.

- *Chapter 5: Design Effective PowerPoint Visuals.* This chapter suggests that you (1) start with your titles, (2) design a basic template, (3) think visually as you design, and (4) edit your efforts.

- *Chapter 6: Refine Your Nonverbal Delivery.* The final aspect of preparing your presentation involves your nonverbal skills—how you look and sound to your audience. This chapter explains how to (1) analyze your nonverbal style, (2) practice your nonverbal delivery, and (3) manage your nervous symptoms.

ACKNOWLEDGMENTS

LR: Thanks to my coauthor and friend Mary Munter whose work has impressed me from the moment I first read it; to NYU Professor, Irv Schenkler, who suggested important revisions; to Jane Seskin, a great writer and advisor; to Lucy Ellmann, a witty novelist with an eye for rogue commas and a talent for saying just the right thing; and to Joann Baney, my extraordinary business partner and supportive friend. I would also like to thank all the Columbia University students who have so cleverly linked what I teach to what they do in the workplace, with a special tip of the hat to Donna Childs—a former business school student who has turned audience analysis into an art form. Thanks also to Aparna Yellai, who has worked diligently to improve every page of this edition. And finally thanks to my *very* supportive family and friends, including my sister-in-law, Judy Russell, who inspires me more than she knows.

MM: I am grateful to the thousands of executives and students I've been privileged to teach; to my colleagues at MCA and ABC; to my coauthor Lynn Russell for her prodigious efforts; and, most of all, to Rob—now and forever (finally!).

We would also like to acknowledge our sources, which are listed on pages 144 and 145 in the bibliography.

Lynn Russell
Professional Development Company

Mary Munter
Tuck School of Business Dartmouth College

About the Authors

Lynn Russell started the faculty development program at Columbia Business School and worked with PhD students and professors to improve their communication skills. She has taught management communication at Columbia for over 20 years, first to MBAs and now in executive education programs. She is also the president of a communications consulting company in New York City and routinely assists executives who want help preparing or delivering presentations.

Over the past three decades, Professor Mary Munter has been active in research and teaching management communication, consulted with over 90 corporate clients, and written numerous books and articles. She teaches at Dartmouth's Tuck School of Business and has previously taught at the Stanford Graduate School of Business and various international universities.

Guide to
Presentations

PART I

Strategy Framework

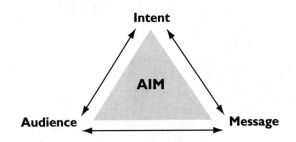

PART I

Presentation Strategy

Many people dislike the idea of giving a presentation. Some immediately start to worry about how they'll look or sound. Others become obsessed with making great visual aids. And others simply procrastinate, figuring they'll just "wing it" or recycle a presentation they've given before. Not one of these choices guards against a major presentation misfire. Nor do they consider the single most important factor in determining the success of your presentation. That factor is presentation strategy.

Applying strategy is the secret to presentation success. Unfortunately, many presenters don't think strategically. They shoot themselves in the foot, so to speak, because they "fire" before they "aim." Many give little thought to their audience, rely on vague or unstated goals, and deliver in-the-moment messages that may not even be suited to a presentation. To avoid this syndrome, consider audience, intent, and message strategy, which we have summed up as AIM:

- **A** = Analyze the Audience (Chapter 1)
- **I** = Identify Your Intent (Chapter 2)
- **M** = Make the Most of the Message (Chapter 3)

As you can see on the diagram to the left, the three AIM components interact. As a result, you won't be thinking about audience, intent, and message in lockstep order; instead, you will discover that each AIM element influences the others. For example, what you intend to accomplish will be based on what you know about your audience. Similarly, which messages you decide to highlight will be linked to what you've identified as your intent.

You may be tempted to begin by thinking about what you'll say, what slides you'll use, or how you'll look and sound, but be patient; each of these implementation concerns is covered in Part II. Instead, start with strategy: avoid a presentation misfire by taking the time to AIM.

3

CHAPTER I OUTLINE

I. WHO ARE THEY?
   1. Start with the primary audience.
   2. Remember the secondary audiences.

II. WHAT DO THEY KNOW AND EXPECT?
   1. Consider what they know.
   2. Check their expectations.

III. WHAT DO THEY FEEL?
   1. Empathize with their emotions and interest level.
   2. Determine their probable bias.

IV. WHAT WILL PERSUADE THEM?
   1. Assess various appeals.
   2. Build support with benefit statements.
   3. Consider your credibility.
   4. Determine how to reach the decision makers.

CHAPTER I

Analyze the Audience

Analyzing the audience is an essential part of presentation strategy. A good analysis requires going beyond your initial assumptions. It involves gathering information about the people who will be listening to and be affected by your talk.

As you analyze the audience, try to do more than just reflect on your past speaking experiences. If done well, your analysis will involve picking up the phone, sending emails, meeting with people who will be in the audience, or talking to someone who is familiar with the group. It will also involve empathizing with the audience—imagining what it's like to walk in their shoes.

Much of what you need to know about your audience can be learned by getting detailed answers to the four questions covered in this chapter: (1) Who are they? (2) What do they know and expect? (3) What do they feel? (4) What will persuade them?

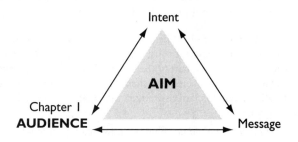

I. WHO ARE THEY?

The first question encourages you to gather general information about
your audience—including demographic data about the group and facts
about individuals. Start with the primary audience, which includes
everyone who will be in the room listening to your talk. And remember
the secondary or hidden audiences: they are the people who will hear
about your presentation or be affected by it, even if they won't be in
the room on the day you present.

1. Start with the primary audience.

The difficulty of your task depends on several variables: the group's
size, where people are located, how much time you have before the
presentation, and, perhaps most significantly, your relationship with the
group. For instance, it's fairly easy to gather information about six
colleagues who work in your office, but when the audience is hundreds of strangers, you will need more time and effort to get answers
to your questions.

When the audience is unknown, begin by locating the people who
can help you with your analysis. Ask questions about the group and
learn what you can about individuals. Keep adding and assimilating
information up to and including the day of your talk.

- *Get inside information.* When you are an outsider—whether you're
  from a different country or just a different department—you need to
  talk to people who are part of the group. If one of these people seems
  especially helpful and credible, then request a follow-up conversation
  so you'll have help clarifying vague information or deciphering conflicting views.
- *Collect demographic data.* Find out how many people will be attending your presentation. Ask about their age range, their educational
  backgrounds, and the types of jobs they have. Gather all the data you
  can, including information about gender, religion, race, and culture.
- *Learn about the group.* Find out how well they know each other, what
  they like in terms of delivery style, whether they have different levels
  of fluency with the language of the presentation, if they tend to be talkative, punctual, informal, and so on.

- *Inquire about individuals.* Discover who knows the most about your topic and talk to that person before your presentation. Also find out who has influence with the group. Try to learn about the decision makers who can say "yes" to your request.
- *Continue collecting information.* You can keep gathering information about the audience even on the day you present. Meet the people who arrive early, watch for reactions to what you say, and listen carefully to the questions people ask.

When the audience is familiar, you will need less help; however, just because you already know many, most, or all the audience members doesn't mean you can skip audience analysis. It simply means the process will be easier and you'll have more time for the difficult parts.

Begin by confirming the demographic data and thinking about the group's traits. However, don't rely on your assumptions alone. Discuss your perceptions with others and use tools, such as assessment instruments or opinion surveys, to get an even better understanding of who they are.

- *Confirm demographic data.* If you know the group well, you can figure out most of the demographic data on your own. Nevertheless, gauge the audience's size either by requesting that people confirm their attendance or by asking the person who's handling logistics about the group's maximum and minimum size.
- *Analyze group tendencies.* Think about what the audience likes and dislikes and how they typically behave. Do they engage in small talk and enjoy humor or do they tend to be all business? Do they like to challenge ideas or do they need to be encouraged to voice their doubts? Will they ask for details or do they dread minutiae? If you don't know this information, talk to people who do.
- *Use assessment instruments.* If your work group has gone through a training program that used assessment tools—such as the Myers-Briggs Type Indicator (MBTI) or Tracom's Social Styles—keep in mind what you know about people's preferences or style, especially if you know this information about one of the decision makers.
- *Consider using an opinion survey.* If you want to learn about their opinions, ask people to fill out a brief questionnaire. Make it anonymous if you're the boss and you want a true assessment of their opinions rather than their best guess about what you want to hear. If the group is large, you can contact a small random sample to get a general idea about the group's views.

2. Remember secondary audiences.

Because they are hidden, secondary audiences are often overlooked. They shouldn't be. These frequently forgotten audience members can influence the effectiveness of your presentation. Therefore, ask yourself: (1) "Who else may hear or see the messages intended for my primary audience?" and (2) "Who else may be interested in or affected by my talk?"

Considering the secondary audience will benefit you in several ways. Your awareness may enable you to reach a decision maker not in the room, send an important message to a wider audience, build support for your ideas, or enhance your reputation as an advocate or expert. This awareness can also give you more control over who hears confidential information. So, at the very least, analyzing the secondary audience should enable you to gain allies or limit leaks.

Gaining allies: Often, presentations have a ripple effect. You deliver your message to the primary audience and they, in turn, share this information with others. To take advantage of this process . . .

- *Ask audience members* to pass along your important messages so others can hear your ideas and understand your views.
- *Create clear handouts* that will make your points for you; encourage people in the room to take and distribute your materials.
- *Reach out to those who will be affected by your recommendations*, such as the people who will end up doing the work. They will be more likely to follow your suggestions if you provide detailed instructions and find a way to emphasize the value of what they're being asked to do.

Limiting leaks: If you plan to present confidential information, recognize the danger of including this information in hard or electronic copy. It's exceptionally difficult to control who will see your printed or emailed materials. Even if you share your confidential remarks only with the primary audience, you may still have trouble controlling who else hears them. One-on-one conversations are better than group venues if your goal is to ensure confidentiality.

II. WHAT DO THEY KNOW AND EXPECT?

Long before you decide what you plan to say, you'll want to find out
(1) what they know about you and your topic and (2) what they expect
in terms of format.

1. Consider what they know.

Think about not only the audience's educational background and work
experience, but also about the topic, the language, and your credibility.

Empathize with the beginners.　To help you determine what will
be new or confusing, remember when the material was new to you.

- *Identify the jargon.* All groups have lingo that is commonly understood within the group. Jargon can become so commonplace that people forget they're using it. For instance, a word as simple as "bus" will
  mean something very different to an emergency medical technician
  than it will to a commuter.

- *Simplify the information.* Focus on the ideas that are essential instead
  of those that aren't needed to grasp the main point. Use familiar
  examples to explain difficult concepts. Try comparing a complex
  procedure to an everyday activity or incorporating several concrete
  examples to make an abstract idea less confusing.

Deal with mixed background needs.　Some of these tips may be
helpful if your audience includes both experts and novices.

- *Open with an informal poll.* At the start of your talk, ask audience
  members about their level of expertise. Experts may be more willing
  to listen to background information once they learn that others don't
  share their familiarity with the subject.

- *Provide background material.* Send the beginners an article or CD that
  provides an overview of the topic or add a glossary of technical terms
  to your handouts.

- *Invite the experts to be part of the talk.* Before the talk, include experts
  by asking their opinion about how to make the material appropriate
  for others. During your talk, ask them to elaborate on one of your
  points, discuss recent examples, or respond to questions related to
  their special knowledge.

Address second language issues.   Here are some techniques you can use to help the non-native speakers in your audience.

- *Check your use of idioms and metaphors.* Common expressions may seem perplexing to someone who's new to a language. So rather than reminding people to "dot their i's and cross their t's," consider asking them to "check the details." Similarly, sports metaphors cause confusion if your listeners aren't familiar with the sport, which means they may not know that a "slam dunk" is a sure thing.

- *Avoid sarcasm and be careful with humor.* Sarcasm depends on vocal tone; it often does not make sense to someone from another culture. Similarly, humor that relies on puns or culturally based information may not be understood.

- *Adjust your delivery.* Enunciate clearly and speak a little slower, especially at the beginning. Use visual aids so people can both see and hear your important points.

Start thinking about your credibility.   Credibility refers to the audience's opinion of you—how they perceive your competence and character. Each audience member will have his or her own ideas about what makes you credible, which means your credibility will vary from one audience member to another and from one situation to the next. Credibility is difficult to assess because even people who know you well will probably be startled if you ask them for an assessment of your competence or character. As a result, you will often be forced to rely on assumptions.

You may want to begin thinking about your credibility by considering these questions:

- Have the audience members met me before?
- If not, what sort of first impressions will they form?
- What have they read or heard about me?
- What do they know about my education and experience?
- Will they view me as an expert on this topic?
- In what ways will they consider me to be similar to them?
- Do they think that I'll be advocating for a cause or position?
- Will they view me more favorably if I discuss conflicting views?

2. Check their expectations.

If you are presenting to people in your department, you are likely to be aware of the group's expectations about format. However, when you are presenting to people in a different culture, each and every aspect of your presentation will be influenced by the cultural context in which you are communicating.

Our definition of "culture" includes factors as wide-ranging as country, region, industry, organization, gender, ethnic group, and work group. The material in this book focuses on giving presentations in a so-called "Western business culture." If you are presenting in another culture, think about how these guidelines need to be adapted to meet those cultural expectations.

Format expectations: Format refers to everything from logistical considerations to communication norms. Ask what's expected in terms of timing, visual aid use, formality, and question and answer (Q&A) sessions. Sometimes, groups will be flexible, caring little if you do something unexpected. In other cases, failing to meet their expectations can cause problems. Don't risk irritating the people you're hoping to influence; if you plan to go against the norm, be prepared to explain why you are engaging in the unexpected.

- *Timing:* Ask how long your presentation should be, where it fits on the agenda, and when breaks occur. You don't want to prepare a lengthy presentation if your audience expects a 10-minute talk.
- *Visual aids:* Find out what's expected and what's possible. You may decide to go with the norm and use PowerPoint like everyone else on the agenda, or you may discover that the group has grown weary of slide presentations and prefers that you do something else.
- *Formality:* Ask how to address members of the audience, what's appropriate in terms of dress, and whether to use an informal or formal delivery style. You don't want to discover, after the talk, that Martha preferred to be called Dr. Stodt or that your interpretation of "business casual" violated the company's dress code.
- *Q&A:* Inquire whether you should expect questions throughout your talk or at the end. Find out how much time to allot for discussion. If the group has a history of posing challenging questions, learn about this tendency so you can prepare.

Cultural expectations: If you are planning to present in a new country, to international visitors, in a different part of the country, or to any group in which you are an outsider, then get assistance from someone who knows that culture. Reynolds and Valentine's *Guide to Cross-Cultural Communication* (2010), another book in this series cited on page 145, covers many relevant issues, including some of the following cultural differences:

- *Perception of time:* Some cultures view sticking to the agenda as a necessity; others have a more limited use for schedules. In addition, some cultures place great value on the past, others concentrate on the present, and still others focus on the future.

- *Differences in motivation:* Some cultures value material wealth and acquisition; others place greater value on relationships, status, or personal growth. Don't assume that your audience is motivated by the same factors that influence you.

- *Image factors:* Some cultures prize wisdom, age, and experience, while others seem more impressed with innovation, youth, and risk taking. Some readily accept women as experts and decision makers, while others tend to have difficulty seeing women in such roles.

- *Expectations about delivery:* Cultural norms determine if you're speaking too quickly or slowly, too loudly or softly, or too much or too little. They can even change the meaning of your gestures.

- *Reactions to colors:* Different groups have different associations with colors. For example, many Wall Street executives associate red with bad financial news. Yet, just a few blocks away in New York City's Chinatown, most business owners consider red a joyful color with many positive connotations.

- *Expectations about space:* Cultures have different norms about how to use space effectively. You might be viewed as "distant" if you maintain too much space between you and your listeners or you might make others uncomfortable if you get too close and violate their personal space. Termed "the hidden dimension" by author Edward Hall, these space boundaries vary by culture.

- *Norms about the communication medium:* Some cultures routinely use email, while others encourage face-to-face hallway discussions. In some organizations, formal presentations are common, while in others they are rare. If you are new to an organization, ask about these communication norms.

III. WHAT DO THEY FEEL?

Business audiences are not driven by facts and rationality alone. So don't merely collect facts about your audience; consider their emotions, interest level and bias, too.

1. Empathize with their emotions and interest level.

To figure out their emotions and interest level, try to put yourself in your audience's shoes.

Gauge their emotions. They may have a range of feelings about you and your message. Some of their emotions may be positive. For instance, perhaps your mentor is in the audience feeling pride and enjoyment. On the other hand, perhaps a rival is also there, experiencing negative emotions such as jealousy and anger. In other cases, the audience's feelings may not have anything to do with you or your talk. For example, if a colleague is scheduled to present as soon as you finish, he may be so worried about his talk that he can't concentrate on yours. Similarly, if audience members are worried about impending layoffs, the stress permeating the room will affect your talk.

Assess their interest level. You will present differently to a highly engaged group than you will to a bored, clock-watching bunch.

- *High interest level:* When interest is high, you can get right to the point. Include plenty of discussion time because people often want to make comments or ask questions about topics that intrigue them.
- *Mixed interest level:* You might decide to open your talk with a "grabber," a technique that creates interest, as explained on page 61. Also be sure to use a few benefit statements as described on page 19. Or you might try breaking the presentation into two talks; keep the required portion brief with an optional follow-up discussion.
- *Low interest level:* In these cases, your first job is to sell them. Use motivational tools, such as grabbers, benefit statements, and the techniques explained on pages 15–17. Rather than lecturing, try to involve the audience in some way. Keep your talk brief so they won't feel as if you're wasting their time. And, if you are delivering a sales presentation, act quickly on any attitude changes that occur as a result of your pitch; such changes may not be long-lasting with this type of audience.

2. Determine their probable bias.

You will want to know as soon as possible if the group is likely to be in favor of your ideas, feel indifferent about them, or be strongly opposed. Their views may be a result of their values, attitude toward change, trust in you, or preference for another option. Often, their bias is also linked to how your request affects them.

Evaluate your request.   Think about what you want the audience to do as a result of your presentation. Are you asking for something time-consuming, complicated, or difficult? Or will it be fairly easy to comply with your request? If you are unclear about what you want, see pages 30–33, which explain how to set a presentation objective. With this objective in mind, you will be able to decide whether you are asking for a little or a lot.

- *Asking for a little:* Even if you are making a simple request that places very few demands on your audience, still point out the value of going along with your request; explain how attending the talk or accepting your recommendation supports their beliefs or benefits them in some way.

- *Asking for a lot:* If you are making a difficult or time-consuming request, try one of these techniques: (1) Make the action as easy as possible. For example, provide a checklist of new procedures so they will be easy to remember. (2) Recognize or reward their effort. For instance, if you are asking people to give something up, publicly praise their willingness to put the team first.

Analyze their bias.   Using what you know about their emotions and probable reactions to your request, consider whether your audience's bias will be positive, neutral, or negative.

- *Positive or neutral:* In these cases, state your conclusions or recommendations upfront and reinforce their importance. You may also want to try briefly presenting and then refuting opposing views to inoculate the audience against other arguments.

- *Negative:* In this case, list their possible objections and use the techniques explained on pages 15–17 to influence their views. In particular, focus on the ask-for-less appeal and try to build off small agreements. If their negative feelings are linked to you, see pages 20–21 for ways to improve your credibility. Also consider meeting with an opinion leader before your talk. If you can turn this person into an ally, then you will have an easier time getting others to agree with your views.

IV. WHAT WILL PERSUADE THEM?

Based on what you've learned about your audience, think about how you can persuade them. We will streamline this exceptionally complex topic by reviewing the ABCs of persuasion: **A**—assess various appeals; **B**—build support with benefit statements; **C**—consider your credibility; **D**—determine how to reach the decision makers.

1. Assess various appeals.

Before you put together a presentation, identify the possible objections your audience may have to your recommendation, product, or cause. Then analyze the various appeals that can help you overcome their concerns. A few common appeals include bottom-line reasoning, benchmarking efforts, consistency reminders, request adjustments, and limited opportunity appeals. All these tools of persuasion have strengths and weaknesses. They include both logical and emotional components. They can be used masterfully or clumsily. To use them well, you need to understand why they are compelling and figure out how to mitigate their flaws.

Bottom-line reasoning: When logic and numbers merge, many business people can be convinced that costs can be contained, the timing is right, and change will be profitable. People who pride themselves on being logical and results-oriented often respond well to these data-driven appeals.

To use bottom-line reasoning, you need to collect quantitative data, analyze it, and develop a logical story line. To use the numbers effectively, the data must be credible, the comparisons compelling, and the forecasts realistic. Always make sure you are able to defend your claims.

The influence of these appeals is tied to the audience's opinion of you. If you take numbers out of context, create misleading charts, or attempt to lie with statistics, then you will harm your credibility and give people a reason to dismiss your efforts. You should also examine all the assumptions that guide your arguments and remember that past performance is not a perfect indicator of future results.

Benchmarking efforts: Corporations have used benchmarking for decades to chart progress or make comparisons. This technique is useful in situations involving change or uncertainty. It requires finding out what others are doing and comparing that information to what your company is doing.

Benchmarking is most effective when you compare your organization or project to ones that are admirable or similar. For example, when looking at "best practices" for campus recruiting, an executive will be most impressed when those practices are used by companies he respects. Similarly, if a governor is trying to decide how much money to budget for disaster preparedness, she may be persuaded to increase the total if she learns other comparably sized states in the region spend much more.

Communication expert JoAnne Yates concludes, "although the fact the 'everyone else is doing it' may not be a very good logical argument, it nevertheless influences some people." For this reason, benchmarking has been labeled "the bandwagon appeal": determine if your comparisons are compelling enough to get your audience to jump on the bandwagon.

Consistency reminders: As persuasion expert Robert Cialdini explains, most people want to be viewed as reliable and consistent. As a result, they often work hard to deliver what they have promised and continue to support efforts they have previously endorsed. In other words, they like to "walk the talk."

There are many ways to use consistency reminders in a presentation. For example, if a CEO has recently praised his organization's values, he will feel the pull of consistency if you can show how your recommendations are linked to those values. Similarly, if you can get your audience to agree "yes, there is a security problem," then they will be more willing to explore solutions to that problem.

Like all other appeals, consistency reminders work better on some people than others. For people who value traditions and tend to resist change, the pull of consistency can be especially persuasive. In such cases, if you position a new idea as part of a continued effort, then you might make an innovation more palatable.

A problem surfaces when people are more interested in new approaches than customary ones. Such individuals might be quick to point out that when circumstances change, their opinions do, too.

Request adjustments: Think about what you are asking of your audience. Sometimes your objective will be so expansive that the audience will object to its scope. Other times, you'll discover that to get the audience's attention, you will actually need to increase the size of your request.

- *Ask for less:* Maybe their concern is "it's just too expensive" or "it will drain other resources." In such cases, consider asking for only a small part of what you really want. For example, suggest a pilot program, recommend a trial purchase, or sign up volunteers for a fact-finding committee. Any of these small steps is a way to get your "foot in the door." Once people have given you an initial commitment, you can use the power of consistency reminders to get them to agree to future appeals.

- *Ask for more:* Sometimes known as the "door-in-the-face" technique, this tactic is the opposite of the previous one. It has you begin by asking for more than you really want. After the audience objects to your overwhelming request, you find out whether they are willing to accept a small part of it. After all, if you are willing to lessen your demands, it seems fair that they should compromise, too. Fund raisers sometimes use this approach, initially asking for a huge donation, but later requesting a more reasonable sum. Clearly there is a danger in playing the back-and-forth game of reciprocal concessions; if the audience feels no need to work with you, they may simply slam the door.

Limited opportunity appeals: When timing is one of the objections, presenters can point to a "small window of opportunity." Deadlines sometimes persuade people to act without all the information they would normally seek. However, some people are willing to flex deadlines to get a job done right. In such cases, you might not get a quick "yes" just by reminding them that time is running out.

The laws of supply and demand kick in when people learn that something is scarce. For example, when items are banned or restricted, they often become more interesting. Similarly, for many people, there's just a certain allure to that which is uncommon. However, even if your idea or product is "unique," some people are too practical to be enticed by things they don't need and others are happy to look for substitutes to your "golden opportunity."

2. Build support with benefit statements.

The acronym "WIIFM" stands for "what's in it for me?" Your audience is waiting for you to answer this question with a benefit statement.

Creating a benefit statement involves three steps. First, you identify all the features of a product or an idea. Next, you think about the audience: the more you know, the better your "audience filter" will be. Finally, you combine what you know about the feature with what you know about the audience to generate a benefit statement that explains what's in it for them.

Step 1: Identify the features.   All products, services, and ideas have many, many features. Features are value-free. They are simply facts about the item or idea you are selling. We'll use this book as an example; here are some of its features: two authors, six chapters, an index, descriptive headings, a section that addresses speech anxiety, and so on. Some of these features could be turned into a benefit statement for you; others may have little or no value to you.

Identifying the features of an idea tends to be harder than generating features related to a concrete item such as a book. Nevertheless, try to identify the facts behind your ideas. For example, a real estate professional may discover many facts linked to his idea of relocating corporate headquarters. Those facts may include that his plan: (1) affects the commute of 3,000 people, (2) can begin next year, (3) involves buying rather than leasing, (4) proposes a site near a train station, (5) includes space for an on-site gym, and so on.

Step 2: Apply an "audience filter."   Once you have identified as many features as possible, analyze them from the audience's perspective. You may discover that some of your features will actually lead to objections rather than benefits. For example, while some members of senior management may be thrilled to have an employee gym, others may consider it a frivolous perk. Your understanding of the audience will act like a filter, allowing you to set aside features that won't be useful and identify those that are most likely to be important to the group. As you assess the value of various features, remember the secondary audience. Some people are not only interested in WIIFM, but also concerned about the benefits for others.

Step 3: Create a benefit statement. Benefit statements explain what's in it for them. These statements can relate to tangible benefits such as profits, bonuses, an extra vacation day, or a gift. They may also involve on-the-job benefits, saving people time, simplifying a complex task, reducing errors, or improving morale.

In some cases, simply noting how the feature leads to one of these general benefits is enough. For example, one feature of this book is its descriptive headings. Their general benefit is that they allow people to skim the content to get a quick overview. Most people realize that skimming can be valuable, so you may not need to offer any other details. Two similar examples appear in the following table.

TURNING A FEATURE INTO A GENERAL GROUP BENEFIT		
Step 1	**Step 2**	**Step 3**
Identify the feature	**Apply an audience filter**	**Create a general benefit statement**
The book includes a **section on speech anxiety**	An audience that includes many nervous presenters	Different techniques work for different people. One of the tips in this section might be the one that helps you sleep better the night before a big presentation.
The plan proposes a **site near a train station**	An audience that includes many frustrated commuters and some people with long commutes	Many employees may be able to commute without cars since one proposed site is within walking distance of a train station.

When you are delivering benefit statements to a group, general ones such as those in the table may be enough. However, at other times, you may need to go the next level, creating a detailed statement that makes it exceptionally clear what's in it for them. The WIIFM focus of benefit statements can be combined with other techniques, such as benchmarking or consistency reminders, to form especially powerful, targeted statements. You can also link these statements to the interests of the decision makers, as we will show you on page 23.

3. Consider your credibility.

Credibility isn't a new concept. Aristotle discussed it thousands of years ago, partially defining it as the combination of a speaker's competence and character. As we explained on page 10, your credibility is based on your audience's perception of you, and this perception varies greatly from one situation to the next.

Based on what the audience knows about you and what you've learned about them, figure out which of the following techniques are appropriate. Be aware that highly interested and motivated audiences are more likely to be swayed by appeals linked to your content than by those related to your credibility. However, for less-interested audiences, credibility appeals may be very important. We've divided these credibility-enhancing tips into two sections: those based on your competence and those linked to your character.

Competence credibility: It's not surprising that if the audience thinks you are competent, they're more likely to accept your opinions. Competence credibility can be associated with everything from the type of information you have on your résumé to the smoothness of your delivery style.

- *Authority:* Sometimes your credibility results from hierarchical power. Having the job of CEO, president, director, or chair may send a signal to some audience members that you deserve their attention because of your role in the organization. Nevertheless, be aware that with some audiences, over-emphasizing your authority can backfire. They may tire of hearing that they should accept ideas just because those ideas have been endorsed by the people in charge.

- *Expertise:* Sometimes your expertise is linked to a title, an accomplishment, or your experience, so be sure they somehow learn that you're a doctor, author, MBA, MPA, or specialist. But expertise is about more than just titles and awards: if you've worked on a project for months, then you may also be viewed as an expert. Likewise, if you've succeeded with other similar projects, then referring to those efforts may bolster your credibility.

- *Associations with experts:* You can also acquire credibility by associating yourself with other people the audience finds competent. Try citing studies done by well-known people at impressive institutions or relating the views of a prominent person. Or, have someone the audience respects introduce you so the audience hears this person's endorsement at the start of your talk.

- *Symbols of competence:* The audience will often link certain symbols to expertise, success, or authority; if you have or wear any of those symbols, then you may acquire some credibility as a result. For instance, gray hair may signal years of experience to some audiences; a uniform with medals may signify authority; or perhaps an expensive watch or designer suit will impress them.

- *Delivery skill:* A polished delivery style can lead the audience to view you as competent—even if your topic has nothing to do with presentation skills. See pages 120–128 for tips on delivery style.

Character credibility: Some credibility appeals concentrate on the audience's perception of your character. For example, Cialdini notes that people prefer to say "yes" to people they know and like. Another element of this type of credibility involves reciprocation and fairness, which has been dubbed "goodwill" by credibility experts French and Raven.

- *Similarity or common ground:* Audiences tend to like speakers they find similar—whether that similarity is reflected in shared values, opinions, needs, experiences, style, or background. Therefore, you can enhance your credibility by referring to a shared experience, mentioning common values or needs, using familiar lingo, or meeting the audience's format and cultural expectations.

- *Good news:* Your audience will be more inclined to like you if you are delivering good news. For example, audiences often respond positively to speakers who compliment them. On the other hand, when speakers are associated with bad news or unpleasant situations, their credibility often suffers.

- *Attractiveness:* Interestingly, many audiences link an attractive image to being both likable and competent. In essence, there is a "halo effect" when speakers are good looking or well-dressed; it causes people to attribute other positive traits to them. Therefore, keeping the audience's expectations in mind, try to dress appropriately and look your best on the day you present.

- *Goodwill:* People often feel a need to reciprocate if you've done them a favor, lent them a hand, or given them a gift. This pattern involves establishing "goodwill." Goodwill credibility also encompasses trustworthiness. For example, if you offer a balanced evaluation of your proposal or acknowledge any potential conflicts of interest, then your audience may see you as fair and trustworthy.

4. Determine how to reach the decision makers.

If you are fortunate, you will already know who has influence with the group. At other times, you will need to identify these people before you can analyze what appeals to them.

Focus on three important roles.   Try to identify the decision makers, opinion leaders, and gatekeepers.

- *Decision makers have direct power or influence.* A decision maker may be easy to spot because she's your boss, potential boss, client, or customer; however, titles alone may not be enough to identify the decision makers. For example, in some cases, decision making may be a group effort and you will want to determine exactly who's on the decision-making team.

- *Opinion leaders shape views indirectly.* Unlike decision makers, opinion leaders don't have the authority to approve your request. What they do have is lots of credibility with the audience and the ability to shape the audience's perception of you and your ideas. Opinion leaders tend to be hard to identify if you are not familiar with the audience. Nevertheless, if you know who they are, keep in mind how and when they might use their influence.

- *Gatekeepers control the flow of information.* If the decision makers are not in the room, you will need to route your message through someone else, known as the gatekeeper. This person has direct access to the people you need to reach. Learn all you can about the gatekeeper to decrease the chances of your message being blocked, misrepresented, or misunderstood.

Consider their preferences.   If you know little about these audience members, then ask others about them and think about what would influence you if you were in one of these roles. Analyzing decision makers, opinion leaders, and gatekeepers is certainly easier if you've presented to them before. In such cases, think about which of your appeals seemed to impress them and which ones they tended to ignore.

Also recall what they've said about their preferences and analyze the appeals they tend to use. Sometimes people employ techniques that they themselves find compelling. For instance, if your boss frequently wants to find out what your competitors are doing, then he might be a fan of benchmarking. If he spends lots of time asking questions about the column charts on your slides, then bottom-line reasoning might be a better option.

Create targeted benefit statements.   You can target your benefit statements so they deliver clear, specific messages that will resonate with various decision makers. The following table uses the example we referred to when explaining benefit statements—the employee gym—and shows how that feature can be turned into several targeted benefit statements, directed at the decision makers in the audience.

TURNING A FEATURE INTO TARGETED BENEFITS		
Step 1	**Step 2**	**Step 3**
Identify the feature	**Apply a decision-maker filter**	**Create a targeted benefit statement**
The plan includes **a new gym**.	For an **opinion leader** who wants to keep costs under control	The gym's cost can be controlled; we'll actually qualify for lower health-care fees once we provide an on-site fitness facility, which means the gym will pay for itself in three to four years.
	For the **decision maker** not in the audience, who recently spoke about her concern for employees' health and well-being	As the CEO recently said, "finding time for our health and peace of mind makes us better employees"; this gym is just one more example our CEO can mention at the next employee meeting to show what we're doing to ensure the well-being of our greatest resource—our people.
	For a **gatekeeper** who wants to show his support for the decision maker	
	For another **opinion leader** who is also a yoga enthusiast	The gym offers convenience; even the busiest employees will be able to take stress-reducing yoga classes either over the lunch hour or after work.

When you think about the ABCs of persuasion, don't think of them in isolation. Remember that all these factors can work together to overcome objections, build support, enhance your credibility, and convince the decision makers to say "yes" to your request.

CHAPTER 2 OUTLINE

I. CONSIDER YOUR GENERAL PURPOSE.
   1. Tell and sell situations
   2. Consult and join situations

II. WRITE YOUR PRESENTATION OBJECTIVE.
   1. Results-oriented and audience-focused
   2. Specific and measurable
   3. Attainable and worthwhile

III. USE YOUR OBJECTIVE TO STAY FOCUSED.
   1. When to write your objective
   2. How to use your objective

CHAPTER 2

Identify Your Intent

In addition to thinking about what your audience wants and needs, part of your strategy involves analyzing what you want and need. Therefore, we call the second element of presentation strategy "identifying your intent."

To begin, think about the task you're undertaking and note the general purpose of your talk. Then, narrow your focus until you can create a carefully crafted statement called "a presentation objective." At first glance, constructing these statements won't seem too difficult. But don't be fooled: writing a presentation objective is much tougher than it seems. You'll need to practice to perfect this skill. Once you do, you'll have a talent that makes you far more efficient and focused every time you present.

So, to identify your intent, (1) consider your general purpose, (2) write a presentation objective that specifies what you are trying to accomplish, and (3) use your objective to stay focused as you put together and deliver your talk.

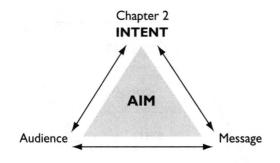

Chapter 2
INTENT

AIM

Audience   Message

I. CONSIDER YOUR GENERAL PURPOSE.

Keeping the audience in mind, think about your task. For example, suppose that at the start of the workday, you have been asked to welcome new employees. If so, you'll have a great deal of control over what you will say and can expect very little commentary from the audience. Also, suppose that later in the day, you are scheduled to meet with clients to hear their reactions to a proposal. In this situation, you'll have far less control over what you will say and when you will say it. Instead, you'll need to encourage your clients to share their views. These two situations demonstrate the trade-off between a speaker's control and the audience's involvement. When you have lots of control, there won't be much involvement. When there is lots of involvement, you won't have much control.

The following diagram makes the same point. The information-sharing or "tell" situations appear at the bottom. They offer lots of control over what is said, but include very little audience involvement. Once you move up to the persuasive or "sell" situations, you have less control and some audience participation. The "consult" and "join" situations feature high levels of audience interaction. They are focused more on working together or building relationships than on delivering a prepared message.

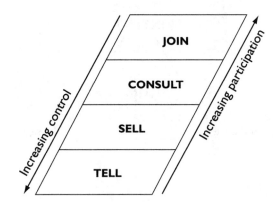

I. Tell and sell situations

Presentations are suited to tell and sell situations—those times when you are an expert or advocate. By their very nature, they give you a fair amount of control over the message and its delivery. Even with lengthy Q&A sessions, they are only moderately interactive.

Tell presentations: If you want to deliver how-to information, welcome new employees, give a progress report, review financial results, or share a memorable moment, you are in a "tell" situation, trying to provide information. Whether your presentation is labeled the weekly update, a financial analysis, a training session, a few opening remarks, or just a story, it is some sort of informative talk.

Most likely, in a tell presentation, you'll determine that your overall task is to explain, inform, review, warn, highlight, update, point out, analyze, compare, or share. If you dig just a bit deeper, you'll uncover your general purpose. For example, perhaps you already know what you want to explain: the rationale for the new dividend policy. Or maybe you've been told what you need to analyze: potential computer security problems. These and other examples of general purposes are listed in the table on page 28.

In reality, most "tell" presentations have a little bit of "sell" in them. For instance, while your general purpose may be to review best practices for campus recruiting, you may also want to encourage the seasoned recruiters to mentor less-experienced personnel. Similarly, if you desire to share your vision for the organization, you may also want to offer several reasons why the audience should embrace that vision.

Sell presentations: When you're pitching a product or trying to change attitudes or behaviors, you're in a "sell" situation. In such cases, you often want your audience to accept your thinking and then do or say something as a result of it. Whether your talk is termed a sales pitch or a motivational message, it's some sort of persuasive presentation.

In such situations, your task may be to influence opinions, initiate change, encourage behavior, recommend a new policy, thwart the opposition, get their approval, or just persuade them to say "yes." If you add a little more detail, then you will know the general purpose of your presentation. For example, maybe you already know what you want to influence: support for wind power. Or maybe you know what you're trying to thwart: cuts to the research budget. These are just two of the sell examples listed in the following table.

EXAMPLES OF GENERAL PURPOSES FOR TELL / SELL SITUATIONS (suited to presentations)	
Types of situations	Examples of general purposes
TELL	• Explain the rationale for the dividend policy • Analyze potential computer security problems • Share my vision for the company • Review best practices for campus recruiting • Highlight the elements of my business plan
SELL	• Motivate employees to build off this year's success • Avoid anticipated cuts to the research budget • Encourage community support for wind power • Pitch our proposal for a new corporate headquarters • Be added to their list of approved suppliers

When you're selling, it's helpful to have at least some audience involvement. Closing a sale is easier when you can hear the audience's concerns and respond to them, which is why many sales presentations include lots of time for audience members to ask questions. In addition, be aware that in many sales efforts, you'll have to involve your audience emotionally, not just intellectually. To get this involvement, you'll need to give up a little control and use persuasive appeals that go beyond bottom-line reasoning.

2. Consult and join situations

Presentations are not suited to consult and join situations—those times when you are really a facilitator, moderator, or negotiator. If you are seeking information, rather than giving it, then you are in a consult or join situation.

Consult situations: Preparing a presentation is not the same as planning a meeting because meetings feature audience interaction rather than the delivery of a prepared message. For tips on how to run a meeting, see *Guide to Meetings*, cited on page 145.

When a presentation becomes highly interactive, it's often the result of Q&A. Typically, in Q&A sessions, the speaker has control when explaining the ground rules and while responding to questions. Yet, there are times when these interactions become far less controlled. For instance, perhaps the speaker announces, "Since you all want to discuss this topic, let's extend Q&A so you can share your views." In this case, the Q&A would be a consult situation.

Join situations: Join situations are even more collaborative. In these cases, other people usually control the message more than you do. For instance, if you were part of a brainstorming session or a team-building retreat, you would be one of several communicators, having little control over many of the messages being sent. These, and the following examples, feature interactive communication.

EXAMPLES OF GENERAL PURPOSES FOR CONSULT / JOIN SITUATIONS (more suited to meetings than presentations)	
Types of situations	**Examples of general purposes**
CONSULT	• Discuss the causes of employee turnover • Get reactions to the strategic plan • Share concerns about a new travel policy
JOIN	• Solve a technology problem as a group • Negotiate a project schedule and tasks • Generate a list of division goals

II. WRITE YOUR PRESENTATION OBJECTIVE.

In this section, we explain how to create a presentation objective that is (1) results-oriented and audience-focused, (2) specific and measurable, and (3) attainable and worthwhile.

Writing such an objective benefits you in many ways. For example, it saves you time by preventing you from researching topics you won't end up using or from making dozens of slides no one will see. It provides clues about how to open and close your talk. And, if some of your presentation time gets cut, it helps you figure out how to adjust on the spot.

1. Results-oriented and audience-focused

A presentation objective is more than a general statement about your goals or a recap of your presentation's purpose. Instead, it's a statement you create for your own use—one that keeps you on track as you put together and deliver your presentation.

Seek results.   Your presentation objective will only be useful if it actually saves you time and helps you evaluate your efforts. Similarly, a business presentation will only be successful if it accomplishes real results. Therefore, from the very beginning, link your presentation to the results you want to achieve. To do so, start with this phrase: "As a result of my presentation. . . ."

Focus on the audience.   Although it's easier to think about what you want to say than it is to pinpoint what you are seeking from your audience, the bottom line is that the results you seek are linked to the audience; you want your presentation to affect or influence them in some way. So to maintain an audience focus, continue your objective with the words: "the audience will. . . ."

Make changes to the phrase as needed.   You can begin with the exact phrase "As a result of my presentation, the audience will," or you can modify it to describe the nature of the talk, as shown below:

> "As a result of my sales pitch, the client will . . ."
>
> "As a result of my welcoming remarks, the new employees will . . ."
>
> "As a result of this update, the Board will . . ."

2. Specific and measurable

You now need to figure out what you want from your audience. To do so, you need to complete the phrase "As a result of this presentation, the audience will" with a list of "targets"—which state exactly what you want your audience to think, feel, or do. These targets should be specific and, whenever possible, measurable.

Avoid vague language. For example, if your general purpose is to "highlight the elements of a business plan," then the presentation objective shouldn't be: "As a result of this presentation, the audience will understand the highlights of this business plan." Instead, as a would-be entrepreneur, you would want to specify which three or four elements you really want to highlight and decide what you mean by "understand." For example, do you want your listeners to be able to describe the talents of the management team to potential investors? Or do you want them to analyze the feasibility of your projections? Or will you be satisfied if they merely recall three important messages about your new venture? And if so, what are they?

Aim for measurable targets. Targets based on emotions or thoughts can be hard to measure in a business setting. By comparison, action-based targets are the easiest to evaluate.

- *Emotions are hard to assess.* In some cases, you can ask people to rate items or share opinions—the way facilitators ask focus group members to record their reactions to speakers, products, or ideas or the way pollsters collect information about preferences and opinions.

- *Understanding is difficult to measure.* Because you can't use final exams or pop quizzes in the workplace, you will have a difficult time measuring what your audience "knows." Unless you have the authority to ask your audience to actually apply or analyze concepts, you may have to settle for identifying the important sound bites and images you want them to hear and see.

- *Actions are the easiest to measure.* Often you will want to specify what you want your audience to "do" or "say." You may decide to have them "complete a sample form" or "authorize a trial purchase." If possible, seek results that can be measured at the end of your presentation or shortly after your talk.

3. Attainable and worthwhile

Your presentation objective should include several targets. Rank their importance and assess their difficulty. Knowing which ones are the most important will help you decide which ones to keep.

Make sure your objective is attainable.   Typically, people think they can cover many more topics or achieve many more results than possible with a single presentation. To avoid this trap, critique your objective by considering how much time you'll really have, factoring in the receptivity of the audience and acknowledging the limitations associated with giving a presentation.

- *Be realistic about timing.* Consider the time you will need for introductions, the time you will spend listening and responding to questions, and so on. Estimate the actual time you will have to accomplish your presentation objective.

- *Use audience analysis insight.* If, for example, you need to build interest or overcome a negative bias, then you will have less time to accomplish your objective.

- *Know what's possible.* Many things you say will not, in fact, be heard and remembered, which is why you need to limit the number of main points highlighted in a presentation.

Make sure your objective is worthwhile.   Once you become skilled at creating presentation objectives, another issue may surface: they can become too straightforward.

Consider this simple objective: "As a result of my presentation, the audience will agree to include us on their approved supplier list." Although it meets the criteria reviewed so far, this objective wouldn't help you decide what to include in your pitch. To make it more useful: (1) identify key messages by inserting benefit statements or specifying take-away points or (2) include "supplemental targets," which might refer to attitudes or emotions. Although tough to evaluate, emotion-based targets don't have to be excluded. If they help you focus, add them as extra targets.

The following table lists four presentation objectives that are audience-focused, results-oriented, specific, and measurable. They were used to prepare real presentations. More importantly, each of them accomplished worthwhile results.

FROM GENERAL PURPOSES TO PRESENTATION OBJECTIVES	
General purpose	**Presentation objective**
Explain the new dividend policy (TELL)	As a result of my presentation, the analysts will hear that we've changed our dividend policy for three reasons: (1) investor attitude has moved toward a yield preference, (2) our continued level of surplus capital made it impractical to continue the current payout ratio, (3) two tax law changes made the new policy more desirable.
Share my vision for the company (TELL)	As a result of my presentation, the VPs will 1. Explain to their direct reports that (a) innovation involves embracing risk and accepting false starts and (b) managing people effectively is both cost-effective and culture-effective. 2. See what I hope our company will look like 10 years from today: an image that features more than two dozen new products on display in our conference rooms and familiar faces throughout the ranks of senior management. *Supplemental target:* The audience will be inspired by anecdotes about the contributions of great managers.
Motivate employees to build off this year's success (SELL)	As a result of my presentation, the employees will 1. Give their applause to our six top performers. 2. Find out that we met our goal and expanded market share .24%. 3. Hear three new positioning messages we'll roll out next quarter. 4. Review a list of promotional tools and compare the number available to the number they currently use. *Supplemental target:* They will feel proud to be part of a successful team and use some new tools to achieve even better results next year.
Be added to their list of approved suppliers (SELL)	As a result of this sales pitch, their purchasing department will 1. Hear that Lite Gauge Metals has (a) a reputation for on-time delivery, which means they won't need to hold excess inventory, and (b) the ability to slit wide-width coils, which means they can reduce lead times for their 55" material. 2. See product samples that verify the precision of our machinery and review packaging protocols that explain why our material arrives without dings or scratches. 3. Agree to add us to their approved supplier list and ask us to provide quotes for at least two different specs this quarter.

III. USE YOUR OBJECTIVE TO STAY FOCUSED.

Your presentation objective will help you throughout the presentation process—from the early stages when you are thinking about the audience and researching your topic to the final moments when you are closing your talk.

1. When to write your objective

You will be more efficient if you draft your presentation objective before you do substantial research. Although audience and intent both need to be considered early in the presentation process, different people like to proceed in different ways. In most cases, you will need to be flexible as you approach strategy; you may discover that you'll need to modify your presentation objective before you determine what you'll say.

Draft your objective early in the process.   Some people draft a presentation objective before they do anything else. Others begin with audience analysis and then move to intent, using a system that mirrors the sequence of this book. And still others use their general purpose as a springboard to collect information and then write their presentation objective. If you are having trouble drafting your presentation objective, use a mind map or another tool to help you get started.

- *Using a mind map:* This tool is popular with random thinkers. It can help them generate, focus, and synthesize information. You will find information about mind maps on pages 54 and 59.
- *Trying another focusing technique:* Other tools can help you identify your intent. Several are described on page 56.

Make modifications as needed.   Situations change, and your presentation objective may need to be changed, too. For example, you may discover a new computer virus is crippling computers in other parts of the world, so your warning about computer security now needs to focus on how to prevent this specific hazard. Or you may learn that people outside the company plan to attend your presentation, so you can no longer include and highlight confidential information. Although the presentation objective is supposed to keep you on track as you determine what you'll say, of course you'll need to make adjustments as you discover new information.

2. How to use your objective

Your presentation objective keeps you focused as you prepare and present. It also enables you to determine your success.

As you prepare: Keep your objective in mind as you put together your talk. Consider it when you . . .

- *Prepare your opening and closing:* As explained on pages 38–40, the first and last parts of your presentation are most likely to be remembered; therefore, make sure your opening and closing are linked to your presentation objective in some way.

- *Decide what to highlight:* If your presentation objective identifies a sound bite that you want the audience to hear, use one or more of the highlighting techniques described on pages 42–43 to ensure this message gets emphasized.

- *Design your visual aids:* Not all your information can or should be included on your visual aids. As explained on pages 79–81, your slides, deck pages, or handouts should emphasize what's important, and much of what's important is the information that helps you accomplish your objective.

As you rehearse and present: Your presentation objective helps you determine what to cut and what to emphasize. After a timed rehearsal, you may discover you have too much information; if so, a clearly defined presentation objective shows you what to eliminate. Your objective also helps you stay on track when you are answering questions or running overtime. For example, if a question is related to your presentation objective, then you'll want to comment on it thoroughly, making your response of interest to the whole group. On the other hand, if a question is not linked to your objective, then you'll want to address it quickly, but not allow it to sidetrack you from what you are trying to accomplish.

To evaluate your success: You made sure your objective was measurable for a reason: so you can evaluate your efforts. Just because your boss said, "Hey, you looked good up there!" doesn't mean your presentation was a success. Similarly, a momentary stammer or audiovisual glitch doesn't doom you to presentation failure. Remember, the way you succeed is by setting a good presentation objective and then meeting it.

CHAPTER 3 OUTLINE

I. MAKE YOUR MESSAGE MEMORABLE.
  1. Harness the power of beginnings and endings.
  2. Chunk your content.
  3. Use highlighting techniques.

II. CONSIDER THE MEDIUM.
  1. Compare presentations to other options.
  2. Supplement your presentation with another medium.

CHAPTER 3

Make the Most of the Message

Now that we've addressed audience and intent, we'll focus on the third part of AIM: message strategy. Although the term "message" has many meanings, as part of the AIM model, it refers to the content of your presentation: what you include in your talk, how you structure this content, and how you emphasize the points you want to make. It also refers to the "medium" you are using to deliver your content—in this case, a presentation.

The medium influences how information is received by your audience, which is one reason that message strategy is connected to audience strategy. In addition, "message" is very closely linked to "intent"—your objective should be suited to the medium you are using, and it should clearly identify the content you wish to emphasize.

This chapter explains how to make the most of the message. To do so, (1) use techniques to make your content memorable and (2) make sure that a presentation is, in fact, the right medium to use.

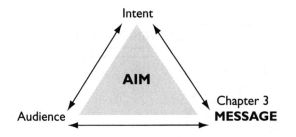

I. MAKE YOUR MESSAGE MEMORABLE.

Although your audience may try to listen to all your data, examples, facts, and opinions, in reality, they can only take in and recall a small portion of what you say. As the speaker, it's your job to help them hear, see, and remember your important points. To make your message memorable, (1) harness the power of beginnings and endings, (2) "chunk" your content, and (3) use highlighting techniques.

1. Harness the power of beginnings and endings.

Audience attention tends to be high when you begin your presentation, but, as you continue, attention may wander. Some people tune in and out, others fall prey to long bouts of daydreaming, and still others get more involved with text messaging than they do with your talk. Nevertheless, when you say something such as "to wrap up . . ." or "so, in conclusion . . . ," most audience members perk up. They listen intently, hoping to find out what they missed along the way.

    Not surprisingly, how your audience listens also affects what they remember. The following Audience Memory Curve is a graphic representation of a well-known principle (sometimes known as the "primacy/recency effect"): people tend to recall what's first and last, not what's in the middle. This principle means the audience is likely to (1) remember what you say during the opening and closing parts of your presentation and (2) recall the first and last items in each bullet list more than those in between.

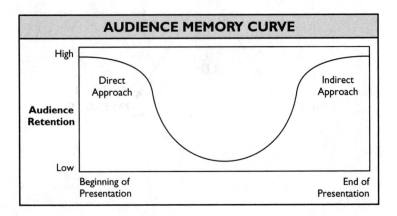

To harness the power of the beginning, emphasize your conclusions by using what's known as a "direct approach" whenever possible. If the audience or message makes this option problematic, then use an indirect approach instead.

Emphasize conclusions.   Your conclusions should be in the opening or closing of your talk. If you share them fully in the opening, you will be using a direct approach.

- *Direct approach:* The direct approach states your conclusions clearly from the onset, so the audience knows your bottom line before they listen to your explanations, details, or arguments. When the audience hears your conclusion first, they have a much easier time following your supporting ideas.

- *Indirect approach:* By contrast, the indirect approach saves the most important conclusions for the end. This approach is like a mystery story: it takes a long time for the audience to determine where all the evidence is leading.

Use the direct approach whenever possible.   Although it may seem counter-intuitive to share your conclusions first, most business audiences prefer this approach because it . . .

- *Improves comprehension and saves time:* People assimilate content more readily when they know the conclusions first. Surprise endings are fine for mystery readers, but not for busy executives who may resent every minute they spend trying to figure out what you're trying to say. The direct approach communicates your position more quickly and effectively than an indirect one.

- *Focuses on the audience's interests more than your discovery process:* The direct approach emphasizes the results of your analysis. By contrast, an indirect one reviews the steps of your analysis. Although many audience members may want to hear about the scope of your project or the ideas that guided your efforts, most will care far more about your final results than about how you discovered them. With a direct approach, you focus on the audience's interests rather than your methodology.

The direct approach is appropriate for all nonsensitive messages. In addition, it's a good choice for sensitive messages if (1) the audience has a positive or neutral bias, (2) they are results-oriented, or (3) your credibility is high. In the United States, chances are you should be using the direct approach more than 90 percent of the time.

Use an indirect approach with caution. Since the indirect approach is harder to follow and takes longer to understand, use it with care. In some situations, it may prevent the audience from disagreeing with you right away, soften their resistance to an unpopular idea, or increase their tendency to view you as fair-minded. Nevertheless, use this approach only when certain constraints require you to do so . . .

- *Audience and message constraints:* when you have (1) a highly sensitive message, low credibility, and a negatively biased or a hostile audience or (2) an analysis-oriented decision maker who insists upon it.

- *Cultural constraints:* when you are presenting in another culture in which the direct approach would be viewed as inappropriate or pushy.

2. Chunk your content.

Another way to help people grasp important ideas is to limit how many you include. Psychology experiments have shown that people can't easily remember more than five to seven items. This finding does not mean that you should stand up, make five points, and then sit down. Rather, it explains why you need to learn how to organize information so that it's easier to recall.

Chunking improves recall. Packaging information into sections, or chunking it, dramatically improves attention and retention. Therefore, you may be able to cover dozens of topics in your presentation if you can find ways to categorize them. Identify your major concepts. Figure out how they are related. Then chunk them into the main sections of your presentation.

Although many people can remember seven items on a list, don't make your listeners work so hard: use anywhere from two to five main sections in your presentation, then divide those sections into a limited number of subsections.

Chunking creates mini-memory curves.   A major benefit of packaging information in sections is that by doing so, you can add emphatic locations to the Audience Memory Curve. Instead of having one long curve with a big dip, you create several mini-memory curves, each with its own dip and peaks. In essence, chunking elevates overall attention and gives you more opportunities to emphasize important points.

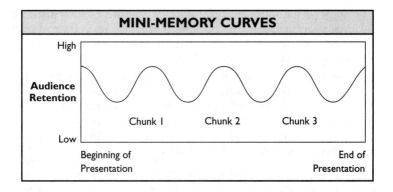

Chunking enables you to create a "preview."   A preview, sometimes called an "agenda" or "overview," lays out the structure of your talk. In other words, it acts like a roadmap, showing the audience the route you will travel as you deliver your presentation. The preview is extremely important for your audience, because listeners, unlike readers, can't flip back and see what they missed. Instead, they rely on what you tell them about the sections, or chunks, that make up your presentation's structure.

All presentations need a preview, but before you can create one, you'll need to identify and label the sections of your talk. See page 61 for more details and examples of previews.

3. Use highlighting techniques.

In addition to relying on the power of beginnings and endings and chunking the content, you can also use other techniques to emphasize information. This section identifies seven highlighting tools that can capture the audience's attention and make your message memorable.

Repetition gets noticed.   People remember what they hear or see several times, so one way to highlight a point is to repeat it.

- *Say your sound bite more than once:* If you have a catchy statement you want the audience to recall, say it more than once. Or repeat that idea in another way, perhaps adding an example or showing an image that makes the same point.

- *Always repeat to reinforce structure:* You can also use repetition to reinforce your presentation's structure. The preview you include in your opening uses this technique: the audience hears the sections you'll be covering during your opening and then once again when you begin each section. Transitional statements, as explained on page 64, also use repetition to reinforce structure.

Flagging signals importance.   The technique of "flagging" is easy to use. You simply draw attention to important points by using a verbal flag, such as "If you remember only one thing, remember . . ." or "Here's the critical point. . . ." No matter which words you use as a flag, they should signal that an important idea is coming up next.

The unexpected grabs attention.   People tend to remember something that is unusual or unexpected—called "the Von Restorff effect," after the psychologist who researched this phenomenon. By using a surprise or attention-getting change in your presentation, you can focus the audience's attention on a point that would otherwise be lost. For example, try telling a startling story, dramatically changing your delivery style, showing a powerful video clip, or altering the pace of your presentation in a humorous or unexpected way.

Yet, here's the caveat: with both flagging and the Von Restorff effect, the more you use these techniques, the less emphasis each use will have. Even more problematic, a surprise or change that is seen as too gimmicky may damage your credibility and, at the same time, make this damaging moment very memorable.

Visuals provide reinforcement.   During a presentation, the presenter is the most important visual; nevertheless, well-designed visuals can also make a presentation more memorable. If people see a message as they listen to it, they are more likely to retain it. To apply the Von Restorff effect further, if one visual is different than all the rest (for instance, a photograph rather than ubiquitous bullet lists), then the unusual visual will be the one that's remembered.

Involvement adds interest.   Because people tend to drift off as they listen, you may want to involve the audience so they're doing more than just listening: ask them to think about a single question or discuss a relevant point, have them participate in an exercise or demonstration, give them a chance to talk to each other by forming "buzz groups," or set up some other type of group activity. Although such activities take time away from your prepared content, they can help you achieve your objective. Typically, audiences recall what they heard, saw, and experienced when they were highly engaged.

Breaks help people focus.   If you're planning a long presentation, understand the value of scheduling a break. Most people can't sit and listen for two hours; in fact, research shows that people tend to lose concentration after 50 minutes without a break. So, you will get more accomplished if you devote at least 15 minutes of your two-hour talk to a break. If used properly, a break turns a long talk into two manageable presentations, giving you more opportunities to position important messages at the beginning and the ending. Schedule breaks so they come between (not in the middle of) main points.

Mnemonics assist memory.   These devices have long been used to help people retain information. Some are rhymes, while others use visual and auditory links to improve memory. One common type, an acronym, makes a word out of the first letters of items in a list. For example, we use the acronym AIM to stress that strategy involves **A** (Audience), **I** (Intent), and **M** (Message). Since AIM summarizes our entire approach to presentation strategy, we hope this mnemonic device makes the concept more memorable.

II. CONSIDER THE MEDIUM.

Always be sure that a presentation is the best medium (or "channel") for delivering your message.

1. Compare presentations to other options.

You have many channel choices. You can write an email, pick up the phone, set up a conference call, deliver a presentation, and so on. In this section, we'll offer some tips about choosing the most effective channel.

Variations among the options: Some of the choices are written and others are spoken. Some reach groups, while others target individuals. In addition, some are no tech or low tech, while others rely on new technology and remind us that even more sophisticated options are likely on the way.

- *Written versus spoken:* Written options include emails, memos, reports, and text messages, while spoken ones include phone calls, meetings, panel discussions, and presentations, just to name a few. Unlike most spoken options, written media create a permanent record, and many are capable of delivering detailed messages that can be easily edited. But writing doesn't include nonverbal elements, such as vocal traits or body language.

- *Group versus individual:* In addition to presentations, group media include conference calls, meetings, websites, and blogs. These are less private than meeting with an individual, phoning someone, or sending a personal letter.

- *High tech versus low tech:* High-tech alternatives include video conferences, electronic meeting systems (EMS), web pages, and webcasts, while low-tech options include face-to-face conversations and traditional written correspondence. Using technology can add "noise" or elements that distort both verbal and nonverbal messages. For example, videoconferences can include static that interferes with vocal cues and camera shots that make facial expression hard to see. Nevertheless, high-tech options enable people in different locations to communicate more rapidly than they could with low-tech ones.

A presentation, then, is a spoken, group medium that is traditionally low tech, but one that can be supplemented with high-tech visual aids or written materials.

Channel-choice checklist: What you know about your audience and intent should influence whether you give a presentation. Other factors—such as privacy, logistical constraints, cost, and content—may also play a role. Use these questions to assess your options:

1. *Does your audience have a preference?* If your boss or client tells you that you are giving a presentation, then chances are, you're giving a presentation. In other situations, the decision may be up to you. If so, assess the audience's preference and consider the advantages and disadvantages of using that medium.

2. *How much audience participation do you want?* Presentations are suited to tell and sell situations, which offer lots of control, but limited audience interaction. If you want higher levels of participation, include a Q&A session in your talk. If you need even more participation, arrange a meeting instead.

3. *Do you want nonverbal communication?* (1) If nonverbal messages and interaction aren't important, then you may be able to communicate in writing, which is less expensive in terms of audience time. (2) If vocal cues would be helpful, but body language isn't important, then use a teleconference. (3) If rich nonverbal cues are important, then choose a face-to-face medium, such as a presentation. Nonverbal elements such as prolonged eye contact, a clear vocal tone, and a firm handshake can help establish credibility, build relationships, and correct miscommunication.

4. *Do you want to control the timing of the message and response?* Consider whether you need to know exactly when your message will be received or to control when, or even if, you will get a response. Face-to-face options offer the most control over these factors.

5. *Do you want a permanent record?* Written and recorded efforts leave documentation. If you need to retransmit your message, then an electronic record will be helpful. If you don't want a record, avoid written channels and opt for unrecorded telephone or face-to-face interactions.

6. *How much detail do you want to communicate?* Writing can include charts, tables, diagrams, and photographs as well as words. You can include a great deal of detail in a written report or on a website; if you tried to include the same level in a presentation or meeting, much of it would be lost since people can process more information through their eyes (reading) than through their ears (listening).

7. *Do you need to control costs?* Meetings and presentations frequently cost more than people realize, especially if the event is held at an off-site facility. To reduce the expense, some people opt to write, while others choose to meet or present using video or teleconferences.

Presentation advantages and disadvantages: Each medium involves trade-offs, whether you're giving up some control to get more participation or whether you're sacrificing privacy so that many people can hear the same information at the same time. The following table identifies several features of a presentation and explains the benefits and drawbacks of each feature.

PRESENTATIONS ADVANTAGES AND DISADVANTAGES		
Presentation feature	**Advantages**	**Disadvantages**
High control of content/ low audience involvement	• Meets your needs when you are an expert or advocate wanting to inform or persuade • Provides control over what content is addressed and how and when it is delivered	• Fails to meet your needs when you want to gather information, work as a team, and so on • Limits audience participation, which can lower interest level and attention
No record (unless recorded or supplemented with handouts)	• Limits information leaks • Can be supplemented with slides or handouts to provide a record	• Makes it hard for people who didn't attend to find out what they missed • Allows information leaks (if the supplemental materials include confidential information)
Face-to-face and group medium (audience and speaker in the same place at the same time)	• Enhances verbal messages with rich nonverbal cues • Enables speaker to make clarifications right away • Allows speaker to seek an immediate response and to measure success based on the presentation objective • Saves time compared to a series of one-to-one meetings • Gets people out of their offices and focused on your presentation	• Limits detail (listeners different than readers) • Prevents speaker from avoiding angry audience members • Allows decision makers to say "no" in a public forum, which makes it harder to influence their views later • May involve high costs or scheduling problems • Lacks privacy, making it difficult to deliver sensitive or hard-to-hear messages to specific audience members

2. Supplement your presentation with another medium.

If a presentation alone won't accomplish everything you want, then consider supplementing it with another medium. For example, if you add written materials, you will be able to include detailed information or document your talk. Likewise, if you need more interaction, then maybe you will choose to include a Q&A session. Or maybe you will want to think of your presentation as part of a larger effort, using other types of communication before and after your talk. All these possibilities enable you to capitalize on some of the advantages of giving a presentation and overcome a few of the drawbacks.

Adding written materials: Writing has several advantages over speaking. (1) It's suited to complex information because it can be viewed and reviewed at the recipient's own pace. (2) It leaves a record that can be saved in a computer or file cabinet. (3) If electronic, it can be easily and inexpensively distributed to a large audience.

If you choose to supplement your presentation with written documents, you can use them as background material sent before your talk, pass them out during your talk, or distribute them after the presentation, either to provide additional information to interested audience members or to serve as a permanent record. Two common types of presentation materials are handouts and decks.

- *Handouts:* If you need to discuss complex financial information, you might distribute a spreadsheet at the point in your presentation when you are discussing those numbers—instead of projecting a table of microscopic type on your slide. You might also use handouts as background material—distributing reports, articles, or URLs of relevant websites before your talk. Or you might want to prepare take-away handouts, such as lists of resources, articles you referenced, or brochures about your organization, service, or product.

- *Decks:* Chapter 5 presents more information about this common visual aid, which can be used in different ways. (1) Decks may be the primary visual, in which case, the speaker and audience move through the printed material together. (2) At other times, they are used along with projected slides. In these instances, the presentation deck may simply be printed copies of all the slides, with or without additional material. Such decks may be distributed before the talk (enabling the audience to use them for taking notes) or after the talk to provide a record of the presentation.

Including some interaction: Q&A sessions make your presentation more interactive. Sometimes audience members ask questions throughout your talk, and sometimes Q&A takes place after your prepared remarks. These sessions can be low-key exchanges or very spirited debates. So when you are thinking about what you want to say to your audience, also consider whether you want to include Q&A, and if so, how you want to handle it; see pages 67–75 for more information on how to do so.

Layering your communication efforts: You may not want to think of a presentation as an isolated event; many times it will be one link in a larger chain of communication. For all sorts of reasons, you might choose to combine several efforts, using one after the other. For example, you might decide that your objective is too complex to be accomplished with a single presentation or you might fear that you're going to face a hostile audience. Just analyzing an unknown audience will probably require you to use another medium to collect the strategic information needed to prepare your talk.

- *When the presentation should be the last step:* If you want to make a big change, such as restructuring your organization or moving a company's headquarters to a new location, then schedule a series of information-gathering meetings before your presentation; you will want to learn what others think and discuss their concerns before you prepare your presentation.

- *When a presentation is just the first step:* Sometimes, you won't have enough time to accomplish your presentation objective in one presentation. In such cases, consider piggybacking several efforts to achieve the results you're seeking. Consider using follow-up presentations, meetings, or written reports.

- *When the audience has a negative bias:* If you fear you'll be confronted by a hostile audience, then try arranging private meetings with influential audience members before your talk. Listen carefully to their objections and views. Try to uncover areas of mutual agreement and get a modicum of support before you present to the group; once the group hears that people they respect share some of your views, you'll have an easier time with those who oppose your efforts.

- *When you need to do extensive audience analysis:* If you're analyzing an unknown audience, you will probably need to layer channels as part of your AIM strategy. For example, to learn about a large, unknown group, you might need to send emails, pick up the phone, and then meet with someone who's familiar with the group.

Once you've confirmed that a presentation is, in fact, the right communication medium for your situation, you can move from strategy to the implementation phase, as discussed in the second half of the book. However, never forget to base that implementation on your AIM strategy: Audience, Intent, and Message.

PART II

Implementation Framework

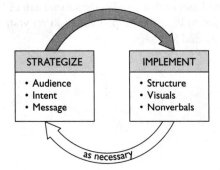

PART II

Presentation Implementation

W hen most people think about giving a presentation, they tend to focus on the implementation skills we will cover in Part II: What will I say? What will I put on my slides? How will I look and sound? We hope we have persuaded you by now that you should AIM before you start preparing your presentation. Strategy should always drive implementation. For example, your audience should influence your nonverbal delivery; your credibility should affect what you decide to say; your intent should determine what you choose to put on your visual aids.

The diagram for Part II, shown on the facing page, illustrates this concept: the dark gray arrow shows how your strategy drives implementation. However, because we don't want to imply that this is a lockstep process (that first you set your strategy, then you implement it), we use the white arrow to remind you to refer back to your strategy, as necessary, while you . . .

- Structure the Content (Chapter 4)
- Design Effective PowerPoint Visuals (Chapter 5)
- Refine Your Nonverbal Delivery (Chapter 6)

CHAPTER 4 OUTLINE

I. COLLECT, FOCUS, AND ORDER INFORMATION.
   1. Collect strategic and topical information.
   2. Focus what you've collected.
   3. Order the content.

II. DECIDE WHAT TO SAY.
   1. Decide how you'll open.
   2. Plan a well-organized body.
   3. Determine how you'll close.

III. PREPARE FOR Q&A.
   1. Get ready for their questions.
   2. Refine your listening skills.
   3. Respond effectively.
   4. Listen for challenging questions.
   5. Control difficult or hostile audience members.

CHAPTER 4

Structure the Content

Your presentation strategy (AIM) should influence what you say during your presentation. To structure your content: (1) collect, focus, and order information; (2) decide what to say during the opening, body, and closing of your talk; and (3) think about how you will answer any questions your audience might ask.

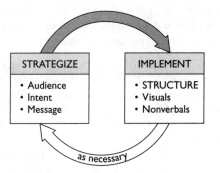

I. COLLECT, FOCUS, AND ORDER INFORMATION.

An effective presentation is based on sound strategy and pertinent information; therefore, devote energy to collecting, focusing, and ordering the information you will include in your talk.

1. Collect strategic and topical information.

To collect information about your strategy and your topic: (1) determine what you already know and (2) research to learn more.

Determine what you already know.   Often you will know a lot about both the topic and your audience; even when the subject matter is new and the audience is unfamiliar, chances are you'll have at least some awareness of the subject and the situation.

- *Review your strategy.* List what you already know about the four audience analysis questions outlined in Chapter 1. Identify your general purpose and write your presentation objective as described in Chapter 2. In addition, think about the benefits and drawbacks of giving a presentation to make sure you're using the right medium for your message, as discussed in Chapter 3.

- *Do a topical data dump.* List relevant facts about your topic and identify some of the resources you want to consult. Round up the data, images, and files you want to reexamine. Jot notes about your ideas and the ideas of others that will guide your approach.

- *Try a mind map.* A mind map is a way to collect and focus topical information all at once. This technique has you (1) write your purpose in the middle of a large sheet of paper and circle it; (2) jot down ideas that are related to what you've put in the circle, using words, phrases, or even simple drawings to quickly capture what you know; and (3) draw lines to connect ideas that are linked. Mind mapping appeals the most to people who are random thinkers. It's a fast, messy way to generate ideas so you can see some possible order in all your free-flowing thoughts. We have included a picture of a simple mind map on page 59. You can learn more about this technique by reading Tony and Barry Buzan's book, *The Mind Map Book*, listed in the bibliography on page 144.

Research to learn more.   You will probably be researching both
strategic and topical information. In your audience analysis efforts,
you may be contacting people familiar with the group or learning
more about where people work by checking a website or company
brochure. You can also research topical information in various ways.
Some people like to work with colleagues who can help them collect
and interpret data. Others prefer solitary research—studying spreadsheets, looking through files, or surfing the web. To make the time you
spend on the internet more productive, refine your searching skills:

- *Internet tutorials:* General internet searches often turn up thousands
  of hits unless you know how to narrow your request. For tips on how
  to navigate the web, check out the UC Berkeley tutorial: http://www.
  lib.berkeley.edu/TeachingLib/Guides/Internet/FindInfo.html. This
  site even explains how to find "the invisible web."

- *Tip sheets:* If you don't have time to become an internet maven, at
  least spend some time learning more about how to use various search
  engines. For example, if you are using Google, check out their tip
  sheet at www.google.com/help/cheatsheet.html.

2. Focus what you've collected.

At this point, you should have gathered lots of information about your
topic. Some of it might be articles or notes about other people's views.
Some of it might be numbers such as a surprising statistic or a stack
of spreadsheets. It's now time to sift through all the comments and
facts and to figure out exactly what those numbers mean.

Assess the information.   Using your AIM strategy, look at the
information in two ways: based on how the audience will respond to
it and how useful it will be in terms of your presentation objective.

- *Based on the audience:* Decide what information will be new and
  interesting to the audience. Think about how it might influence their
  views. Highlight any information that might help you create statements that can explain what's in it for them.

- *Based on your intent:* Use your presentation objective to separate
  what is on target from what's not necessary. Some presenters like to
  post their objective near their computer so they can keep their eye on
  it the entire time they are collecting and focusing information.

Adjust as necessary.   Perhaps some of the information is too complex, too basic, or not relevant for your audience. If so, you'll need to simplify it, find better information, or make other adjustments. If you have the authority, you might want to change the composition of the group. For example, if you have one expert and many novices, you might warn the expert that she'll find the presentation too basic for her needs or ask her if she would like to assist you in presenting some of the material.

In other cases, the information you collected might seem appropriate for the audience, but you can't figure out how to use it to accomplish your objective. If so, you might search for more material, modify your objective a bit, or try to focus your ideas in another way.

Try other focusing techniques.   Experiment with the following techniques; some of them have you write down your ideas, while others involve talking about your topic.

- *Nutshell the information.* Writing expert Linda Flower suggests that you focus your ideas by capturing the essence of what you are trying to communicate in a few short sentences—or in her words, in a "nutshell."

- *Try the email technique.* This tool builds on the nutshell technique by having you turn those short sentences into an email. For example, assume you have to explain the gist of your presentation to someone who isn't able to attend. Concentrate on this person as you draft an imaginary email. How would you briefly describe your point of view? What key take-away messages would you include?

- *Teach your ideas to someone.* Some people prefer talking to writing; they have an easier time clarifying their thoughts if they have a live audience. To use the teaching technique, sit with a colleague and ask him if you can talk about your upcoming presentation. Explain why your colleague should care about the information and how he can recall the most important points.

- *Use the elevator technique:* This focusing tool is adapted from "the Hollywood pitch," used by screen writers to sell their ideas to busy film executives. The elevator technique has you imagine that you are speaking to the decision maker. Pretend you have this person's attention for 90 seconds, while you are taking an elevator down to the lobby. What messages would you most want to share? What would you ask for before the elevator door opens?

3. Order the content.

To organize the pertinent information you've collected, find a method for grouping similar ideas so you can discover the chunks of information that you will include in your presentation.

Using an outline: If you think in a very linear fashion and you can easily distinguish major themes from secondary points, then you will probably prefer to organize your ideas with an outline: either a traditional one (using Roman numerals and capital letters) or an informal one (using bullet points and dashes). As we discussed in Chapter 3, limit the number of major sections in your outline and order your points in a way that will seem logical to the audience and help you accomplish your presentation objective.

Making an idea chart: Frequently used by consultants, idea charts are more visual than outlines. To create one, (1) list your important ideas, (2) find ways to group them into a limited number of categories, and (3) label each group. If constructed like a pyramid, your main idea will be in a box at the top of the pyramid, with your main sections placed below it, as illustrated on the following page. For more information about how to construct idea charts, refer to Barbara Minto's book in the bibliography on page 145.

Starting with a storyboard: This ordering method may prove useful for visual thinkers. To create a storyboard, (1) start with a series of blank boxes that represent possible slides; (2) create a preview slide that identifies the sections of your talk or save this step for later if necessary; (3) sketch the images you want to use in various boxes; (4) write important messages as headlines; and (5) number the boxes to show the sequence. Create your storyboard with pencil and paper, not in PowerPoint, where you may waste time perfecting slides that you later decide to delete.

Using your own method: If the above suggestions don't seem helpful, then find a method that works for you. For example, you might try using a combination of mind mapping, as described on page 54, and a pad of sticky notes. Aided by these tools, you could use the mind map to identify important ideas and then transfer those ideas to sticky notes. The notes could then be moved around until they form an idea chart that shows how to order your talk.

IDEA CHART EXAMPLES

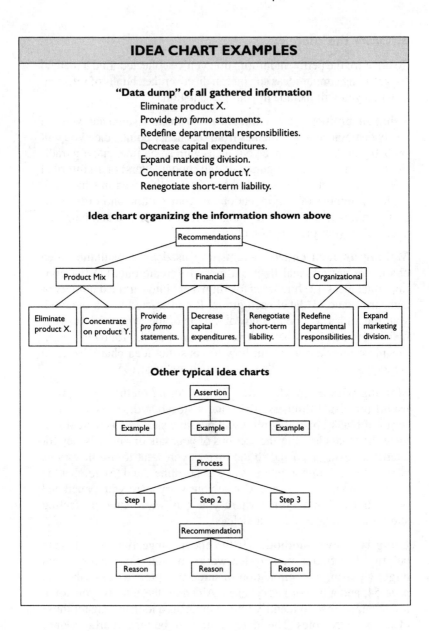

"Data dump" of all gathered information
Eliminate product X.
Provide *pro formo* statements.
Redefine departmental responsibilities.
Decrease capital expenditures.
Expand marketing division.
Concentrate on product Y.
Renegotiate short-term liability.

Idea chart organizing the information shown above

Recommendations

Product Mix | Financial | Organizational

Eliminate product X. | Concentrate on product Y. | Provide *pro formo* statements. | Decrease capital expenditures. | Renegotiate short-term liability. | Redefine departmental responsibilities. | Expand marketing division.

Other typical idea charts

Assertion

Example | Example | Example

Process

Step 1 | Step 2 | Step 3

Recommendation

Reason | Reason | Reason

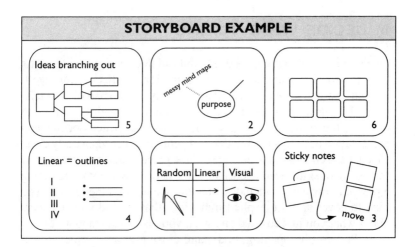

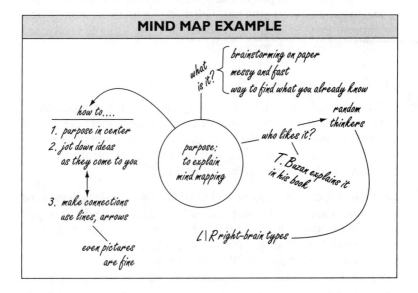

II. DECIDE WHAT TO SAY.

Once you've researched, focused, and ordered the information, it's time to turn that material into a presentation. In this section, we'll explain how to decide what you'll actually say in each part of your talk.

Like a written document, a presentation has three parts: the opening, the body, and the closing. But, unlike a written document, a presentation needs a structure that is repetitive and exceptionally clear. Listeners aren't like readers: they can't glance back to refresh their memories or skip ahead to check out the end. So when you are giving a presentation, always include a preview that outlines the sections you plan to cover and use explicit transitions that remind your listeners about what you just covered and what you plan to talk about next.

Prepare the opening, body, and closing in any sequence that works for you. Some people like to start with the body and their preview to ensure a clear structure. Others prefer to use a chronological approach, first deciding how to open, then preparing the body, and finally determining how to close.

I. Decide how you'll open.

Your opening is crucial. It sets the stage, builds interest in your topic, and explains the structure of your talk. Although there are several tasks to accomplish with the opening, don't make this section too long or complex; be sure you get to your preview well before the audience wonders where you are headed with your talk.

Set the stage.   Use the opening to connect with your audience and introduce the scope of your presentation. For instance, in some persuasive talks, you may use the opening moments to explain your position and how it shapes the way you'll be approaching your presentation. Or, perhaps you'll include a modified version of your objective so the audience knows what you plan to accomplish. If you are unknown to anyone in the audience, you may also need to introduce yourself so you can establish some credibility.

Grab their attention.   When people are not particularly interested in your topic, get their attention by using a "grabber."

- *Ways to get attention:* You can ask the audience a question, make a promise about what your presentation will deliver, describe a vivid image, tell a brief story, or explain why the audience should care, perhaps telling them exactly what's in it for them.
- *Techniques to use carefully:* Humor can easily grab attention, but make sure it fits your personality. Like all other attention-getting techniques, humor needs to be appropriate for the audience and related to the situation. You also want to make sure it won't make anyone in your audience feel picked on or left out. In addition, be careful with grabbers that don't actually grab much attention—like long dictionary definitions read off a slide.

Always include a preview.   An essential part of your opening is the preview. It provides an outline of what you will be saying or, in other words, it tells them what you're going to tell them. It's also a good place to let people know how long you plan to speak.

- *Explain the structure.* If you are following a direct approach, which we explained on pages 39–40, make your conclusions obvious when you give the preview. If you are using a less common, indirect approach, you still need to make the structure clear; however, you will save your main conclusion for the end.

  Example of a preview statement using a direct approach

  In the time remaining this morning, I want to explain the benefits of the new system. First, I'll demonstrate how these new guidelines will save you time; second, I'll point out how you can use them to respond to client's billing questions. And finally, I'll explain how they address a complaint many of you had about the old system.

  Example of a preview statement using an indirect approach

  In the next 30 minutes I want to discuss two topics. First, I'll describe the record-keeping problems that have plagued our billing system. Second, I'll share three options we have in dealing with them.

- *Show them while you tell them.* Feature your preview on a slide or deck page. When you deliver your preview statement, take your time. Direct the audience's attention to the visual so they can see and hear your message.

2. Plan a well-organized body.

If you want people to remember the content of your talk, your points can't be randomly delivered; they need to be presented in a limited number of chunks. By limiting yourself to two, three, four, or possibly five sections, you help the audience follow along.

If you are unsure about how to order your ideas, look at some of the following patterns to find out whether any of them would work for your talk. After you know how you want to organize the body, then you can work on your transitions—how you will wrap up one section and introduce what comes next.

Ordering informational talks: Maybe you have a few key points you need to emphasize or several questions you need to address. Or maybe you are comparing items and want to show how they relate. No matter what pattern you select, keep it simple. For example, select four rather than nine main points or simplify a seven-step process into a three-step one. The following examples show various ways to order an informative talk.

- *Key points:* Identify your most important take-away points and arrange them so you can easily connect one point to the next. Putting the most important point first or last is usually a good idea (for all of the reasons we discussed related to the Audience Memory Curve on pages 38–39). As an example, suppose you have identified three reasons why changing your dividend policy was a smart decision and you want the analysts who follow your company to hear those reasons. To make your message clear, you could order the key points as follows: (1) investor attitude moved toward a yield preference, (2) our surplus capital made the former payout ratio impractical, and (3) tax code changes made the new policy more desirable.

- *Key questions:* Using key questions is less direct than stating key points; however, organizing your talk so it responds to the audience's questions is another common pattern. You might use the "what, why, how" structure: what I'm recommending; why it's necessary; how it can be implemented. Or you can use actual questions, such as the ones that follow, which are four key questions about a new business plan: (1) Why is the environment right? (2) What is our competitive advantage? (3) How will we secure start-up funds? (4) Who will lead and manage this new venture?

- *Steps in a process:* With this pattern you use a chronological approach. For example, if a real estate executive is reviewing the steps her company has and will be taking to improve its relationship with the community, then she might organize her presentation based on three steps: (1) participate in local events to raise the company's profile and build relationships; (2) solve zoning issues by working with people in the neighborhood; (3) create more public space for those in the community.

- *Items or ideas to compare:* With this pattern, you present several items or alternatives, comparing each one to those that came before. For example, if the VP of human resources at a research center wants to explain why certain college degrees are desirable for various positions, then he might organize his talk as follows: (1) PhDs for senior research positions; (2) MPAs for policy research; (3) MBAs for economic research and financial posts; (4) other degrees for grant writing and non-research positions.

Ordering persuasive talks: When you are trying to persuade people, it's easiest to use a direct approach. For example, you may want to organize your talk based on your recommendations—which means the audience will hear these key points as soon as you list them in your preview. Another common way to order a sales pitch is based on the benefits of your product or idea. If you are forced to use an indirect approach, consider the problem/solution pattern, which describes a problem, then shares possible solutions.

- *Recommendations:* If you have lots of recommendations, group them into three or four major themes so they will be easy to recall. For example, if you have a long list of suggestions about how a resort can achieve a four-star rating, then group them into a few topics: (1) listening to our guests, (2) providing service as a team, (3) creating a sense of luxury, and (4) enhancing our reputation.

- *Benefits:* You can also try to sell your ideas, products, or services by highlighting their benefits. For example, if you were speaking as an advocate for wind power, then you might list these benefits: (1) provides high-paying jobs to people in the community; (2) generates safe, carbon-free energy; and (3) makes financial sense because of government subsidies.

- *Problem/solution:* This indirect approach enables you to get people to agree that there is a problem. Next, it analyzes ways to solve that problem. For example, to recommend a costly and unpopular computer security system, you might use this pattern: (1) cyber-security issues and (2) three approaches that heighten security.

Moving from one section to the next: Transitions are statements
that link the sections of your talk. No matter what type of pattern you
use to order the body, you need to include clear transitions that reinforce this pattern. Always remember that listeners have a hard time
paying attention and, unlike readers, they can't go back and review
what they just read. Unless you remind them, some people won't
remember what you are listing.

- *Use explicit transitions:* Avoid vague segues such as "second" or
  "finally." Use detailed ones instead: "A second benefit of wind power
  involves the environment . . ." or "Let's turn to our final recommendation, which focuses on how the resort can enhance its reputation."

- *Take a look backward:* Before you rush to introduce your next point,
  remind people of the section you just finished. For example, "The economic boost provided by high-paying, local jobs isn't the only reason to
  support wind power; a second benefit. . . ." Or, "Now that we've shared
  several suggestions about how to enhance the luxury of our grounds,
  hotel, and restaurant, let's turn to the final recommendation. . . ."

- *Use "backward-look/forward-look" transitions:* If you use explicit
  language and link the previous section to what comes next, you will
  create a clear and helpful segue—a "backward-look/forward-look
  transition." Although you may feel as if you are being too repetitive, your listeners will appreciate these detailed reminders that
  reinforce your structure. These transitions will help daydreamers
  get back on track and alert attentive listeners that something new is
  coming up next.

Examples of backward-look/forward-look transitions

Now that I've highlighted the benefits to our environment (**backward
look**), I'll move to my last point—why the government subsidies make
this investment too good to pass up (**forward look**).

So it's clear that we need to do a better job listening to our guests
(**backward look**), but we also have to change the way we work, which
brings us to the second set of recommendations; they focus on how we
can provide conscientious service by working as a team (**forward look**).

3. Determine how you'll close.

Your audience is likely to remember your last words. Therefore, your closing should be more than just "thank you" or the all-too-common "no more questions . . . well then, that's it." Although you always want to avoid such "dribble" endings, your closing comments can take many forms. We'll give you a few ideas about how to end and alert you to the problem of closing your talk after someone in the audience has asked you a question.

To deliver your closing words effectively, pause and breathe before you say them. Once you have finished, wait a few seconds before you head back to your chair. For more insight about how to use your nonverbal behavior to emphasize a message, refer to Chapter 6.

Closing an informative talk: In an information-sharing (or "tell") presentation, use the final moments to recap what you've told them. In most cases, your presentation objective will remind you what is most important and suggest how to close. For example, your last statement may simply be a sound bite from your presentation objective, or it may be a polished version of how you previously described your presentation using the nutshell technique, as described on page 56. Just make sure there is some connection between how you close and what you're trying to accomplish.

Closing a persuasive talk: In a persuasive (or "sell") presentation, your final comments need to close the sale. Use your presentation objective to help you decide how to craft your closing; try to end in a way that will enable you to measure your presentation's success. For example, you might wrap up by . . .

- *Asking the decision makers* for an order or by requesting authorization to implement your recommendations.
- *Distributing a sign-up sheet* so you can collect the names of people willing to volunteer for your campaign.
- *Restating your most persuasive point* and then arranging to talk privately with the decision maker so you can close the sale during this informal conversation.

Using both initial and final closing statements: If you are planning a Q&A session at the end of your presentation, then you will need two closings. The first one will wrap up your prepared comments and segue into a request for questions. Ideally, the second one will synthesize several pertinent moments from the Q&A session and link them to your presentation objective. If none of the questions can be tied to your objective, then your final closing will be a strong, clear statement, similar to your initial closing. Always make sure the final words the audience hears are yours and that they are linked to your presentation objective.

SAMPLE INFORMATIVE PRESENTATION	
Opening	Introduction of presenter and topic Main conclusions Preview
Body	Point 1 (followed by a backward-look/forward-look transition) Point 2 (followed by a backward-look/forward-look transition) Point 3 (followed by a backward look and segue to closing)
Closing	Summary of points/concluding statement

SAMPLE PERSUASIVE PRESENTATION (FOLLOWED BY Q&A SESSION)	
Opening	Introduction of presenter and topic Recommendation Preview
Body	Benefit 1 (followed by a backward-look/forward-look transition) Benefit 2 (followed by a backward-look/forward-look transition) Benefit 3 (followed by a backward look and segue to closing)
Closing	Initial closing (including a request for questions) Q&A session Final closing (featuring a call for action)

III. PREPARE FOR Q&A.

Don't just prepare for the time you'll be speaking, also think about the interactive moments when the audience will be asking questions.

I. Get ready for their questions.

Decide when to take questions and adopt the right attitude, one that welcomes the audience's participation. Also set aside time to rehearse so you'll be ready to answer whatever people ask.

Decide when to take questions.   You can take questions at the end of the talk or have people ask them throughout. Find out what the audience expects and think about what you prefer.

- *Holding questions for the end:* Ending with questions gives you control of the schedule and flow of information. However, there are risks with this choice: (1) people might be confused if they can't ask questions in the moment and (2) you might find yourself in an awkward situation if people ask questions after you've asked them not to do so.

- *Taking questions throughout:* If people can ask questions during your talk, they can get clarification when they need it. Having interactive moments in the middle of your presentation may also help the audience listen more attentively. However, questions can also upset your schedule and take you off point. To minimize these drawbacks, (1) budget time for questions instead of planning to speak for the entire time you've been allotted and (2) control digressions by using the listening and responding skills described on the following pages.

Value questions.   When someone asks a question or shares a comment, think of it as a compliment—"my audience is interested enough to want a little more detail"—or as a bit of useful information—"now I know my client's views." Adopting this attitude will help you create the right tone for Q&A.

Practice responding.   Anticipate what the audience will ask and practice a few different responses. Have someone help you by posing common questions such as those related to cost, timing, risks, alternatives, and so on. Also ask this person to challenge you with unexpected inquires. If you can record this rehearsal, you will get useful information about how you listen and respond.

2. Refine your listening skills.

Listening expert Robert Bolton breaks listening skills into three clusters of behavior. Use these skills to (1) look like a good listener, (2) encourage participation, and (3) paraphrase the questions you are asked.

Look like a good listener.   Use various nonverbal behaviors to show your audience you are interested in their questions. Check your posture, movement, and eye contact to make sure you appear attentive. Also make sure the atmosphere is right for Q&A.

- *Maintain a posture of involvement.* Face the questioner. Avoid distracting hand or arm placements such as resting your chin on your hand or crossing your arms in front of your chest. Hold your body still: stop any needless movements, such as tapping your feet, clicking a pen, or fidgeting with your notes. Let your body language signal that you're listening intently.
- *Make eye contact.* Look at the questioner, observing her whole face so that you can pick up nonverbal cues.
- *Create an environment suitable for listening.* If appropriate, consider moving to the side of the podium or in front of a table, closing the distance between you and the audience. During Q&A, turn up the lights so the audience can be the focus of your attention.

Encourage participation.   Get people to participate by posing open-ended questions, being silent, and using small signals that encourage them to continue talking.

- *Open the door for questions.* Use open-ended questions that can't just be answered "yes" or "no." Rather than begin with the words "Can you" or "Do you," start with phrases such as "What's your view of" or "Tell me about."
- *Be silent: don't interrupt.* After you've asked a question or invited people to participate in a Q&A session, give them time to think. Wait patiently for at least 10 to 15 seconds so people can collect their thoughts. Don't say anything while you wait. Also, be silent as you listen to their questions. If you interrupt, you won't hear the entire question, and you'll send a signal that you're rushing them.
- *Use minimal encouragers.* Also consider using little cues, called "minimal encouragers," which entice a speaker to continue: nodding, smiling, tilting your head, widening your eyes, or saying "uh huh." As long as these signals are natural, they communicate that you are genuinely interested in listening to the question.

Paraphrase the question. In active listening, a paraphrase is a brief statement that captures the essence of what someone just said. It's a statement that helps people feel heard and one that can prevent miscommunication. If modified a bit, this listening tool can be a great asset when handling questions.

Like regular paraphrasing, Q&A paraphrasing involves more than just repeating what someone said. Instead, a paraphrase translates their words into your own. Both types are brief, but regular paraphrasing focuses on helping the other person, whereas Q&A paraphrasing is used to help you control the interaction and enhance the value of Q&A for everyone in the room.

- *Keep everyone involved:* If someone sitting in the front row asks a question, people sitting in the back may not be able to hear it. Therefore, you need to repeat the question, or better yet, paraphrase it. By doing so, you make sure everyone knows what was asked.

- *Clarify what was asked:* Questions can be hard to understand for many reasons. Maybe the questioner used vague words and created such a long question that you don't know where to begin. Or maybe the question itself was phrased in a way that it seems to be controlling how you can respond. In these situations, a paraphrase can help you deal with the question. Page 72 offers examples of how to paraphrase and respond to challenging questions.

- *Address emotions:* Some questioners let you know how they feel; for example, they may directly state that they are "confused," "delighted," or "extremely worried." Others use only visual and vocal cues to express their feelings. Never forget that these nonverbal cues are part of the question. For example, maybe one questioner's face shows his frustration, while another questioner expresses her irritation with a sarcastic vocal tone. In such cases, you want to paraphrase more than just the actual words. When feelings trump the facts, you might paraphrase by saying something like this: "I recognize that many of you are extremely frustrated by the new paperwork requirements, so let's get to the root of Pat's question: Why do we need to replace a simple, one-page form with this new detailed one?"

- *Diffuse difficult situations:* When you need time to think, paraphrasing can be a great stalling technique. It gives you a chance to gather your thoughts before you respond. Paraphrasing is also a handy weapon in your arsenal if you are battling hostile questioners. For more information about these difficult interactions, see pages 73–75.

3. Respond effectively.

Effective responses help you accomplish your objective. Ideally, they should also be interesting and delivered in a way that keeps your audience involved.

Stay on message.   When you are asked a question, think of it as a chance to make your message heard. To do so, use two powerful techniques: "bridging" and "flagging."

- *Bridging* connects your response to something that is part of your presentation objective. A bridge can be a connecting phrase, such as "which means," or a simple word, such as "and." For example, a bridge might sound like this: "Karla, you've asked an important question about wildlife safety, so I'll address the potential hazards you mentioned *and* explain how we protect birds, animals and plant life at our facilities."
- *Flagging* draws attention to your most salient point. To highlight an important message, use words such as "What's essential to remember is . . ." or "Here's the critical point. . . ."

Balance brevity with interesting detail.   Ideally, your responses will be noteworthy and memorable. You will also want many of them to be brief so you can maintain the interactive nature of Q&A.

- *Make your responses interesting.* Vivid words and well-crafted sound bites are interesting; rambling explanations are not. Stories told in the present tense can bring listeners into the moment; those that plod along chronologically often fall flat.
- *Use brief responses or well-structured longer ones.* If people's hands go up before you finish, either your comments aren't brief enough or you are not clearly wrapping them up. While brief replies hold people's interest, sometimes a question will require a detailed explanation. In such cases, begin with an overview that gives the audience an idea of how you plan to reply and end by using a strong, clear voice, followed by silence, to signal that you are done.

Keep everyone involved.   Paraphrasing the hard-to-hear questions is one way to keep everyone aware of what's being discussed. In addition, call on people from various parts of the room, perhaps alternating from one section of the audience to another as you take questions. When speaking to those in the front, use enough volume so people in the back can hear. And don't just look at the questioner when you respond; focus on other audience members, too.

4. Listen for challenging questions.

Tough questions come in all shapes and sizes, but they tend to fall into three categories: (1) unclear questions, (2) questions framed in a limiting way, and (3) questions for which you don't know the answer.

Unclear questions: Perhaps you've used your best listening skills, but you still have no idea what you've been asked. When a question is unclear, use an "I" response rather than a "you" response. In other words, say "I'm not sure I understand the question" rather than "Your question is confusing." Sometimes the question is only a bit unclear. At such times, paraphrase to check that your assumptions are correct. In addition, be aware of three common types of unclear questions:

- *Vague questions* use nonspecific language. When you hear words such as "it," "this," "that notion," or "the other option," try to clarify your understanding of the vague words with a paraphrase.

- *Long multi-questions* string three, four, or even more questions together. Based on the situation and the questioner, you have several options in dealing with multi-questions: (1) synthesize all the questions and offer a single response, (2) start with the question you like best, avoiding the ones you don't want to address, and (3) answer one part of the question and ask the questioner to remind you of the remaining parts.

- *Broad questions* inquire about huge issues that could never be addressed in a limited time. To deal with them, either narrow the focus and respond to the question or point out the broad nature of the question and offer to address it later, perhaps after the presentation.

Limiting questions: Many types of questions seem to limit your options or lead you toward a response that you don't want to give. They include forced-choice, hypothetical, empty-chair, loaded-language, and false-premise questions. In addition, listen for distorted paraphrases that mischaracterize what you have said.

- *Forced-choice* questions imply there are a limited number of options and ask you to choose one. Often they use the word "or." For example, "What's more important, the amount of time a doctor can spend with each patient *or* the number of patients that can be seen each day?" Remember that "both" choices can be important. Other forced-choice structures ask you to rank items on the questioner's scale or to identify what's "most" significant. Once again, you can reframe the questions so you are setting the parameters.

- *Hypothetical* questions create a situation that doesn't exist, although it could be a potential reality. "If the FDA rejects your application, how will it affect other drugs in your research pipeline?" In such cases, it's best to stick with what is known rather than focus on what might occur. If the questioner is your boss, then you'll likely have to accept the premise; if the questioner is a reporter, then do not speculate.

- *Empty-chair* questions ask you to comment on something said by a third party, someone not in the room. If you didn't hear the CEO's comments or you haven't read the statement put out by the Attorney General, don't even begin to evaluate what was supposedly said or why it was said.

- *Loaded-language* questions include colorful words, phrases, and perhaps even sarcasm that make the question a minefield. Neutralize the language by using a paraphrase. Don't say, "I am not a heartless bureaucrat," instead say, "I know you're disappointed. I wish we had more resources so we could help everyone on the waiting list."

- *False-premise* questions begin with an incorrect assumption: "When did the accounting department begin falsifying their reports?" To respond, correct the assumption: "If you're concerned with the accuracy of our financial reports, let me assure you that we have open books and all our accounting practices are carefully monitored; we stand by our numbers."

- *Distorted paraphrases* aren't really questions; they are inaccurate summaries of your comments. For example, suppose you just finished explaining how your staffing levels would hold steady and someone distorts your remarks by saying: "So you're telling us layoffs are inevitable." Don't ignore these remarks. Correct them by saying, "Let me clarify: our staffing levels will be the same next year as they are this year."

"Don't know" questions: If you don't know the answer, don't bluff. Instead say, "I don't know." Or better, suggest where the person can find the answer. Or better yet, offer to get the answer yourself— "Off the top of my head, I don't know the demographics for that region, but I can easily get that information for you by tomorrow morning." Then be sure you follow up.

In other cases, you may just need a little time to gather your thoughts. If so, here are a few stalling options: (1) repeat or paraphrase the question, (2) turn the question outward by asking the questioner or the entire audience for their ideas and opinions, (3) take a moment to reflect by saying something such as "Daniel, let me think about your question for a second," or (4) write the question on a board or flipchart so that you can discuss it as a group.

5. Control difficult or hostile audience members.

Occasionally, audience members don't have your best interest at heart. They may try to take control of the discussion, attack you or your ideas, or distract you in some way. If so, you need to control the situation without letting the confrontation get personal. Here are some techniques to handle hostility.

Types of difficult questioners and audience members: Different behaviors annoy different people, which means we can't possibly list all the ways audience members can be difficult. Nevertheless, here are a few of the troublesome types and how you might handle them:

- *Pontificators* enjoy the sound of their voices. They ramble on and on, sometimes never even asking a question. To respond, listen intently so you can paraphrase something of value and then bridge to a message that gets you back on track.

- *Nitpickers* focus on minutiae and take you off message. You can acknowledge that "yes, the actual figure is 14.89 percent" and then explain that you would like to focus on trends rather than on specific data points during your talk.

- *Needlers* use sarcasm or try to belittle you in some way. Don't mimic their sarcastic tone or try to embarrass them. Just restate your opinions calmly and clearly, using logical reasoning to back your views.

- *Distracters* initiate side conversations, roll their eyes, or mumble disapprovingly under their breath. You can move toward people having side conversations or pointedly wait until they stop talking, but don't become overly confrontational. Focus on the people who are interested instead.

General tips for handling a hostile audience member: How you manage the interaction between you and a hostile questioner will depend on many variables. For instance, you would deal differently with a hostile boss than you would a nasty colleague. Yet, in all cases, you want to maintain your credibility by being scrupulously polite, trying to find points of mutual agreement, using effective listening skills, and connecting with the audience members who are willing to be fair.

- *Be polite,* even to the rudest audience members. For example, don't snap at a pontificator by saying "So, what exactly is your point?" Of all the tips for handling difficult audiences, being polite is the most important.

- *Lessen hostility* by agreeing to disagree and pointing to common ground. For example, say something such as, "We don't seem to agree on how to handle this customer service problem, but since we agree that we want to do what's best for our customers, we can begin by conducting an assessment of their needs and views."
- *Paraphrase the feelings behind the question.* If the nonverbal behavior implies that there's more to the message than the words alone indicate, acknowledge the questioner's emotions in your paraphrase by noting the anger or frustration.
- *Stop repeat offenders tactfully,* perhaps by putting up your hand and explaining, "I'm sorry to interrupt, but I want to make sure we end on time, so let me touch on the issue you mentioned by saying. . . ."
- *Look elsewhere afterward.* After responding, do not direct your eye contact toward the difficult questioner. If you do, you're just inviting this person to make another challenging comment. Instead, look at the friendly faces so you can avoid repeated volleys with the troublemaker. Also be sure to look at supportive faces when you finish your talk; you don't want to invite another outburst during the closing moments of your talk.

Differences based on interpersonal style: Communication expert Joann Baney suggests that you analyze your own interpersonal style to get some ideas about how you are likely to fare in a hostile Q&A environment. In *Guide to Interpersonal Communication* (cited in the bibliography on page 144), she differentiates between two types of assertiveness: a telling style and an asking style. Knowing your tendencies will help you determine how to respond to hostile questioners.

- *A telling style is direct.* People with this preference are talkative. They tend to use above-average volume and forceful or large gestures. In addition, they don't shy away from conflict. When engaged in hostile exchanges, they can become (1) autocratic, barking orders to people in the room, or (2) challenging, using their quick wit to launch verbal grenades at difficult audience members.

   If you have a telling style, don't label a situation "hostile" too quickly. Be careful not to interrupt, yell, or point at the hostile audience member. Remember, as soon as you verbally attack someone in the audience, you usually lose credibility. Once your credibility is lost, it's hard to get it back.

- *An asking style is less direct.* Someone with this preference tends to talk less and make fewer direct requests than someone with a telling style. In addition, an asking style is characterized by lower-than-average volume, a tendency to listen intently, and a desire to avoid conflict. If your style is more "asking" than "telling," don't hold yourself back, waiting to make sure someone is truly being difficult; by the time you have made this judgment, the audience has likely made the same determination. Therefore, once you sense hostility, immediately use techniques to help you disengage from the trouble-maker, such as holding up a hand to stop a pontificator. Force yourself to correct anyone who incorrectly paraphrases your comments. And remember to keep your volume loud enough so you aren't drowned out by the hostile people in the audience.

If you used both strategic and topical information to structure your content and prepare for questions, you should now have an effective opening, body, and closing for your presentation. You should also have a good idea about the questions the audience will ask. Next, we will turn to designing your visual aids.

CHAPTER 5 OUTLINE

I. START WITH YOUR TITLES.
   1. Identify what the audience needs to see.
   2. Create titles that clarify your message.

II. DESIGN A BASIC TEMPLATE.
   1. Establishing a color scheme
   2. Making typography decisions
   3. Choosing simple backgrounds and layouts
   4. Using company templates

III. THINK VISUALLY AS YOU DESIGN.
   1. Data-driven charts explain the numbers.
   2. Concept diagrams depict ideas.
   3. Photographs add interest.
   4. Animation clarifies complex slides.
   5. Text charts list important details.

IV. EDIT YOUR EFFORTS.
   1. Verify that the structure is clear.
   2. Enhance the visual effect.
   3. Proof and proof again.

CHAPTER 5

Design Effective PowerPoint Visuals

Not all presentations use visuals, but many do, with the two most common options being projected slides and bound pages, known as "decks" or "pitchbooks." Slides are the more formal choice and presenters usually stand while they use them. Decks are often selected for smaller audiences or more interactive situations.

Most presentation visuals are created using PowerPoint. When using this software to design your slides and deck pages, we suggest that you (1) start with your titles to save time and focus your efforts; (2) design a basic template to give your visuals a unified, uncluttered look; (3) think visually to create slides and pages that interest the audience; and (4) edit your efforts to make sure they deliver messages that are clear and correct.

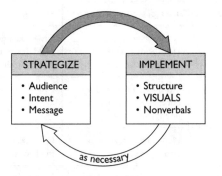

There are several types of decks. Some are used throughout a presentation, with people flipping through the pages together. Others are more like reports, distributed before meetings and used to guide discussions. This chapter focuses on slide shows and the type of deck used as the main presentation visual, with you and your audience looking at the pages together. If you are trying to decide whether to use a presentation deck or slides, we summarize some of their differences in the following table.

COMPARING DECKS AND SLIDES		
	DECKS usually . . .	**SLIDES** usually . . .
Formality	Less formal (Everyone is seated around a table.)	More formal (The presenter stands; others are seated.)
Audience size	Smaller	Larger
Audience focus	Discussion-centered (deck as starting point)	Speaker-centered (slides as back up)
Cueing method	By page number and by referring to elements on charts, diagrams, and lists	By appearance of new slide and by using animation to build content
Preview visual	Table of Contents page	Preview/agenda slide
Design issues	Challenging to design (The "Slide Master" is not set up for decks.)	Easier than decks (Add design elements with restraint.)
Detail	More detail than slides, but much less than documents	Limited detail
Fonts	Medium-size titles and smaller text	Large titles and medium-size text
Charts and diagrams	Can be more complex, can't use "build"	Must be simplified, can use "build"
Last-minute changes possible	No	Yes

I. START WITH YOUR TITLES.

You have already decided what to say. Now you need to determine what the audience needs to see. This section encourages you to list your titles before you begin making your slides or pages. It also introduces an important tool in your design kit—message titles.

1. Identify what the audience needs to see.

In our experience, we find that more presenters make too many visuals than too few. And even worse, they often try to cram too much on the ones they do make. The number of slides or deck pages you will use depends on the situation. However, no matter what the situation, only design slides and deck pages that (1) reinforce the structure of your talk, (2) emphasize your main messages, (3) draw attention to supporting points, or (4) help you respond to important questions. Also search for times *not* to use visuals—moments to keep the audience's attention focused solely on you.

Reinforcing the structure: One good reason to use slides or deck pages is to help the audience understand the structure of your talk.

- *Title slide or deck cover:* This visual highlights your name and the title of your talk. It should also introduce the color scheme and graphics used on later visuals.

- *Preview visual:* One of the most important slides or pages in your presentation is the preview visual. It may be an "agenda slide" that highlights the sections of your talk or your deck's "table of contents" page. Because it is so important, make your preview visual stand out. Give it a descriptive title—more than just "Agenda" or "Overview." Include words that will emphasize the focus of your talk. (We provide more information about creating titles, starting on page 82.)

- *Section visuals:* To clarify the structure of long presentations, you might also want to create section visuals, which are slides or deck pages that mark the beginning of a section. In a deck, you would use one of these visuals for each section listed in the table of contents. In a slide show, you would insert a copy of the preview slide at the start of each section. For more information about how to use a preview slide as a section visual, see page 113.

- *Executive summary deck page:* Some companies require a deck to include an executive summary. This page highlights conclusions or recommendations and explains the scope and flow of the deck. Don't use such text-heavy summaries in a slide show; find other ways to emphasize your conclusions or recommendations.

- *Closing visuals:* As explained on page 66, you may have two closing messages if you plan to take questions after your talk. You may decide to use a visual for one, both, or neither of these moments. A closing visual could focus on synthesizing your recommendations or highlighting a message that captures the essence of your presentation. In a slide show, it could be visual reminder of your main points or it could be nothing—just a black slide that allows you to move in front of the screen. Ask yourself exactly what you want to communicate during the final moments. That message should influence what you want the audience to see at the end of your talk.

Emphasizing main messages: For many presenters, limiting important messages is much more difficult than listing them. However, if you are having trouble generating a list of titles to turn into visual aids, try one or more of the following:

- *Look at your presentation objective for clues* about what needs to be seen as well as heard. For instance, if your objective identifies a sound bite you want the audience to remember, then you might want to use those words as a title on a visual aid. If you haven't done so already, you would also need to decide where this sound bite fits within the structure of your presentation.

- *Recall the focusing techniques* described on page 56. If you used something like the nutshell or email techniques, then you may find important messages embedded in those summaries. If so, think about how those messages fit with the other titles you want to turn into visual aids.

- *Try making a storyboard,* as discussed on page 57. If you already used this ordering technique, then you have sketches that represent possible visual aids. If you haven't done so already, create a headline for every storyboard box. Do those headlines make essential points? If so, add them to your list of titles; you will want to use them, along with the storyboard sketches, as a starting place for various slides or deck pages.

- *Focus on each section* or chunk individually. Sometimes identifying the main messages is easier if you break the job into smaller parts. Work first on whichever section seems easiest and then tackle the more challenging parts.

Drawing attention to supporting points: Some of your main messages might need extra visual emphasis. If so, think about the secondary points that support them. Backup visuals can be based on messages about quantitative data, examples, essential details, or benefit statements that explain what's in it for them. Resist creating a blizzard of backup points. Instead, be selective. Decide which points will (1) provide the strongest support and (2) make the most powerful visuals.

Preparing for Q&A: Maybe you think the audience will have a question you can address, but would rather not unless they bring it up. If so, think of a succinct message that supports your response and turn that message into a Q&A visual. In a slide show, these visuals are typically placed after the closing slide; in a deck, they appear in an appendix. The audience's interest will determine whether you use them.

Making yourself the visual: Sometimes the best visual is no visual. When you are giving a presentation, you may spontaneously decide to break away from your visuals to connect with your audience. Such moments can also be planned. For example, you can insert a black slide in your slide show or create a speaking note that reminds you to put aside the deck. Consider taking a visual aid break for one of these reasons:

- *To fix the flow:* Ideally, your list of titles will have a logical flow. If it doesn't, you can change a message, cut one, add one, rearrange the list, or plan to fix the flow yourself by taking attention away from the visuals, connecting with the audience for a reason, and then segueing back to the visuals.

- *To add emphasis to an important section:* Section visuals provide a good place to stop and take a real break, but they are also an easy place to take a visual aid break. For example, you might set the deck aside and tell a story that sums up the importance of the previous section or start a new section by explaining why you are passionate about what's coming next.

- *To give the audience a change of pace:* Critique your list. Imagine what sort of image will result from each title: is the message most likely to become a chart, diagram, photo, or bullet list? If you spot a sequence that has too many lists or one that bombards the audience with charts and numbers, you might want to cut a title or plan a visual aid break, a place where you will communicate directly to your audience, without support from a visual aid.

2. Create titles that clarify your message.

Some slides and deck pages use "topic titles," which are words or phrases such as "Strategy," "Our Vision," and "Recommendations." These titles tell people what is being discussed, but they don't tell them what to see. On the other hand, more effective "message titles" specify your point, speed up information sharing, and help your visuals make "stand-alone sense." They should also influence how you design all of your slides or pages.

Specify your point: Look at the following column charts. The first one uses a topic title: "Home sales by quarter." It lets the audience decide what point the image is making. The second chart shows the same data, but this version uses a message title. It tells the audience exactly what to see. The chart could have had many other message titles, such as (1) home sales are increasing, (2) sales more than doubled in the second quarter, (3) home sales were steady from April through September, and (4) first quarter sales were exceptionally low. Notice that all these message titles include a verb. Sometimes just adding a verb and a little detail will make your point clear.

Example: ineffective topic title   *Example: effective message title*

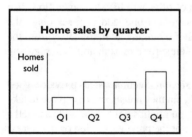
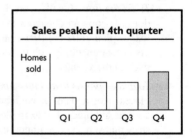

Speed up information sharing: Titles are large, often boldface, and should be placed where the audience looks first—at the top of the slide or page. If they contain a message, then that message will influence what viewers see as their eyes move around the rest of the screen or page. Once your audience sees your main point, they have an easier time taking in the details.

Message titles tend to be longer than topical ones; however, don't make them too complex or they will fail to do their job. For example, if everyone is reading a 15-word title, then no one will be listening to you. Therefore, limit the length of your message titles. You can create titles that wrap to a second line, but in general, strive for brevity—the briefer the better, as long as the title communicates your point. The following table shows how a vague topic title can be switched to a more descriptive one.

FROM TOPIC TO MESSAGE TITLE	
Vague topic title . . .	**. . . transformed into a clearer message title**
Agenda: Bard Real Estate	Build Bard's Community Connections
Recommendations	Follow Four Steps to a Four-star Rating
Summer Web Traffic	Web Traffic Soared in June
Budget Allocation	Salaries were 30% of the Budget
Survey Results	The Economy was the #1 Concern
Experience vs. Sales	Experienced Brokers Sold More Bonds

Create stand-alone sense: Your visuals should make sense even when you aren't there to explain them. The first step in achieving this stand-alone sense involves using message titles. All of your titles should make a clear point and help explain the rest of the content on the visual. When they do their job, such titles aid the audience.

- *Help viewers follow along:* Because message titles explain the main point, they help latecomers understand the context of what they are hearing. They also assist the daydreamers who want to reconnect with the current focus of your talk.

- *Provide useful records*: PowerPoint files that make sense on their own are more useful than those that don't. For example, in some organizations, people use pages created for one presentation in other decks. Seeing a clear title will help others decide whether your deck page delivers a message they want to send, too.

Influence design decisions: The PowerPoint defaults are set up for extremely large titles. We explain how to make adjustments for message titles in the next section. However, other design choices should also be based on your message titles.

- *Create images that match your message.* Your title helps you decide whether a chart, diagram, drawing, map, or photograph will best communicate your point. For example, on pages 100–102 we show how pinpointing your message enables you to discover what type of chart to use. Similarly, on page 105, we explain the importance of matching the visual message of a diagram to the verbal message in your title.

- *Make highlighting decisions based on the title.* How you use color and graphics should be based on your title. We explain how to choose "spot" and "dimming" colors on page 87 and include some suggestions about how to use arrows or other graphics as highlighting tools on page 114.

Adapt to the situation: Your message title should drive the design of the visual and typically be the first thing the audience sees on your slide or page. However, after you have used a message title to create your image, in some cases, you may want to edit your title or perhaps even delete it.

- *When words are implied:* Sometimes you can cut part of a title, perhaps even the verb, and the message will still be clear. For instance, "Four Steps to Four Stars" grabs more attention than "Follow Four Steps to a Four-star Rating," and it will still guide your design efforts better than "Recommendations."

- *When a less direct message is the better option:* Suppose your boss expects to see the latest sales figures in your deck, so you designed a chart that shows the steep decline featured in your message title. However, if you don't want to be the harbinger of bad news, then do what media trainers have termed "blanding it out." Don't emphasize a message you don't want to deliver. Instead, include the required chart, but use a nondescript title. Similarly, if "Build Bard's Community Connections" sounds a little too direct, then simply change "Build" to "Building." The change will soften the tone, but still let viewers know the focus of your visual.

- *When a slide image works by itself:* Suppose one of the messages you listed is captured by a photograph. In such cases, a title might not be necessary since you found a picture that communicates your point. In other cases, adding a word or phrase on top of the image might be enough to clarify your meaning. If a photo works without a message title, then let it fill up the screen.

II. DESIGN A BASIC TEMPLATE.

Before you insert titles on your slides, find what PowerPoint calls the "Master View." Once you are in this view, you can use the "Slide Master" to help you design slides or pages that look unified, not like a mishmash of unrelated items. Why should you create your own master when dozens of prepared ones are available? The main reason is that many PowerPoint options are full of distracting elements that interfere with your titles, text, diagrams, and charts. Although you can alter them to make them usable, it's just as easy to design your own.

In this section, we discuss color schemes, typography, backgrounds, and layouts for your slide show or deck. We also provide a few tips for working with company-provided templates.

1. Establishing a color scheme

Rather than using the numerous and overly colorful PowerPoint options, we suggest creating your own color scheme. To do so, (1) consider the audience, (2) choose a background color, (3) select visible title and text colors, (4) pick a "spot color," (5) include dimming options, and (6) make sure the colors work together.

Consider the audience.   Before you settle on any color, think about your audience. People do not view or interpret color the same way. Some of their reactions might be based on cultural associations, while others might be more specific to individuals.

- *National, religious, and other cultural differences:* When you are presenting in a new culture, ask how colors are viewed. For example, many people have strong associations with the colors in their county's flag. Colors may also have ceremonial connotations; weddings, for example, are linked with white, yellow, or red in various cultures.

- *Business considerations:* Green is often associated with money in the United States because it is the color of the currency. Red, on the other hand, tends to signify loss, especially to those in the financial sector. Like nations, many organizations have colors, with blue a traditional favorite in terms of corporate logos and green a common choice for ecologically focused enterprises. Choose colors appropriate for your industry and company. If you are new to an organization, be careful not to use a competitor's colors as your color scheme.

- *Color blindness:* Even if your corporate colors are red and green, they won't be the right ones to use on a diagram or chart if your boss can't see the difference. About 5–10 percent of the population can't distinguish between red and green.

Choose a background color.   Traditionally, backgrounds are associated with "cool" colors (such as blue, green, or purple), which seem to move toward the back, as opposed to "warm" colors (such as red, orange, or yellow), which appear to move forward.

In reality, the choice is a bit more complex. The background color depends on the type of visual—whether you are showing slides, using a deck, or coordinating a slide show with a handout. It is also influenced by projection and printing equipment, logo colors, visibility issues, audience expectations, and your preferences. Use the following suggestions to choose a background color for your slides or pages.

- *Projected slides:* You can use a dark background—for instance, black or dark blue. Choosing black will cause the background to blend with the screen, but make the objects on your slide look vibrant. Choosing blue will be a safe option, since it is often used for corporate presentations. Other dark colors also make good backgrounds. For a less formal look, pick a light color, such as white or beige. A white background may add so much brightness to a room that you won't be tempted to dim any lights. However, in some rooms white can pose a problem: if the screen is large and the slides sparsely designed, then a white background can cause an annoying glare. Be careful with colors that are not dark or light; they may not provide enough contrast for your text choices.

- *Decks:* White is a great background choice for printed pages. Light colors, such as cream, beige, or pale blue, are also options. Bright and dark backgrounds are less desirable; they use lots of toner so they are more expensive to produce and can look streaky or faded when the printer's toner runs low.

- *Black and white printouts:* White is the best background choice for handouts. If you plan to use two-sided printing to save paper, then also avoid using large black or dark gray shapes because they will be visible on the back side of standard-weight paper. If you are printing with a laser printer, then you should have no problem using two distinct shades of gray; however, if your deck or handouts are being photocopied, both grays may look the same.

Select title and text colors. You can't read pale yellow print on a white page or see black numbers on a dark blue screen. You need far more contrast to make your words and numbers stand out. With dark blue slides, all the options listed in the following table would work for titles, but some might not be good for other text. (For example, white is a safe choice for regular text on a dark slide; however, bright yellow text could make the details look more prominent than the message title.) For white deck pages, choose black for regular text and save the other options for titles or labels.

CONTRASTING COLOR COMBINATIONS	
For a background that is a . . .	**. . . try one of these title or text colors for contrast**
Dark blue slide	White, peach, yellow, gold, pink, lavender, light blue, light green, aqua, beige, or light sage green. Pale colors will look white.
White deck page	Black, bold colors (blue, red, orange, green, or purple), or dark colors (navy blue, hunter green, brown, maroon, rust, indigo, slate, or teal).

Pick a "spot color." In addition to your background, title, and text colors, choose a spot color—an accent color that will work like a spotlight, focusing attention on your most important ideas. Make the spot color the boldest of your palette. Use it sparingly for items that need attention, such as the center of your diagram. (If you are editing a PowerPoint color scheme, avoid inserting this color as the "Fill" or "Accent Color 1"; otherwise, it will pop up every time you create a box or block arrow.)

Add dimming options. Colors used to dim items do the opposite of spot color: they communicate "look somewhere else." Gray is a safe dimming choice, but other colors mixed with gray may also work. For example, if your spot color is bright blue, then a pale gray-blue might work well for less important items. In a slide show, you may want to dim text on a list. Again, gray is a good choice, but you can also use a variation of your background color. For example, on a purple background, a slightly lighter purple could do the job.

Make sure the colors work together. The color scheme needs to use a limited number of colors that all look good together. To find them, use PowerPoint's "Custom Color Screen," which is shown below.

❶ *The custom color box*: You will find bold, pure colors at the top and more subdued ones lower in the box.

❷ *The white- to- black bar:* Modify the lightness or darkness of your selections with the vertical bar to the right, which adds varying amounts of white or black.

❸ *The sample box:* This box shows the color you have found.

❹ *The RGB values:* Whenever you locate a color you like, write down the numbers in the boxes labeled "Red," "Green," and "Blue," so you can create the color again by using those numbers.

If you need more detailed instructions for using PowerPoint, see *Guide to PowerPoint*, listed on page 145 in the bibliography.

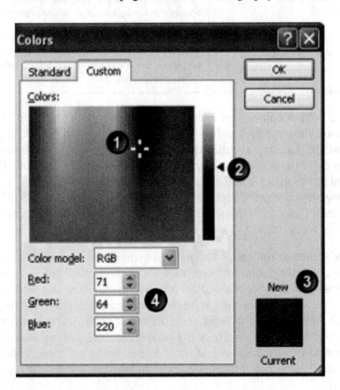

In general, limit your palette to three colors in addition to black, gray, and white. If you opt to use more, avoid what graphic artist Jan White calls "the fruit salad effect"—a kaleidoscope of colors that may look festive, but doesn't make anything stand out.

- *Limit yourself to one dramatic color.* If all the colors are exceptionally vibrant—such as fire-engine red, neon green, and flamingo pink—they will compete with each other and possibly create a juvenile look more suitable for a children's classroom than a company's conference room. Using more than one bold color also makes your job harder; it will be much easier to emphasize your message if other colors don't compete with your spot color.

- *Experiment with less intense colors.* Using PowerPoint's Custom Color Screen, you can transform exceptionally bold colors into more subdued ones. To make colors less dominant, mix them with some gray, black, or white. For example, to make fire-engine red less eye-catching, add some black and you will end up with maroon. To tone down neon green, move your curser down the custom color screen box until you find sage, a mixture of green and gray, which looks more subtle. To soften flamingo pink, just add white.

- *Try complementary colors.* Bold opposites (such as purple and yellow or blue and orange) can be attractive pairings if you make some adjustments. For instance, combine a dark purple background with gold titles and white text or use a navy blue background with peach titles and white text. These combinations offer a high-degree of contrast and provide visual interest.

- *Test deck colors on hard copy.* Prepare a color sample page, using several variations of the colors you have selected. Identify them by the numbers that appear on the custom color screen. Print the page so you can see which variations look the best. If your deck has a colored background, test how each color looks on the background. Save the test page; it may be a useful way to compare colors if your deck is photocopied or produced with a different printer.

- *Test slide colors on the big screen.* If possible, check your colors with the equipment you will be using. If such a test isn't possible, plan to make last-minute adjustments. The colors on your computer will look different than those on the big screen. The biggest difference will be that many colors will seem washed out, so be sure to check them all, paying special attention to light or pale colors, which may just look white. Some colors may even change hues. For example, sometimes yellow looks green on the screen, while peach appears yellow.

2. Making typography decisions

PowerPoint offers more than 100 fonts, but please don't feel obliged to use them all. Some are serif fonts, which have little strokes at the ends of the letters. Others are sans serif fonts, which don't have these flourishes. Many of the other options were designed for posters or party invitations.

You want to choose a very legible font for your visual aids—one that makes it simple to decipher the individual letters. Once you've picked a legible font, you want to use it in a way that makes it easy to read all the words and numbers on your slides or deck pages.

Limit yourself to one or two fonts.   The best way to ensure that your title and text fonts work together is to use the same choice for both. However, many decks use two fonts, one for titles and the other for text. When using two fonts, make sure your choices contrast and complement each other. The easiest way to make them contrast is to choose one serif and one sans serif option. The only way to see whether they complement one another is to experiment; see how they look on a deck page.

- *Serif fonts:* In general, serif fonts create a classic impression. The little flourishes on these fonts tend to make individual letters easy to identify. This enhanced legibility is noticeable on a printed page (rather than on a screen) because printing produces sharp images. However, some serif fonts aren't the best option for text viewed on a screen. Always test those that use thin lines to form all or part of the letters; sometimes the thin strokes are hard to see when the font is projected.

  Example of serif fonts, for a more classic look

  Times New Roman, Cambria

- *Sans serif fonts:* Sans means "without," so these fonts don't have the little flourishes. Their streamlined letter forms make them appear more modern or high tech. A standard sans serif font, like the following examples, can be a great choice for projection, a very good choice for deck titles, and a readable choice for blocks of text in a deck page or handout.

  Example of sans serif fonts, for a more modern look

  Arial, Calibri

Consider the variation among fonts.   In addition to the serif and sans serif distinction, fonts vary in other ways. To do a better job selecting them, learn how to spot several differences.

- *Compare the height of "Example" letters.* Fonts use their height (also known as "point size") in different ways. Some devote much of their height to regular, lower case letters like an "x," while others devote a lot of this vertical space to letter parts that extend up or down, like the low tail on a "p." If you test a font by typing the word "Example," you can compare the height of its "x" to the height of its "p" and "l." The relative size of the "x" is what designer's call "x-height." It has a big impact on how large your font looks. (Verdana text looks bigger than Perpetua because it has a larger x-height.)

    Examples: both 12-point fonts, but different x-heights

    ## Verdana Example

    Perpetua Example

- *Notice letter width and spacing.* Some fonts are wide and rounded, with lots of space between letters. Many of these fonts are easy to read, but they can be challenging to use if you have long message titles or complex labels. Narrow fonts fit into small spaces; however, make sure their condensed spacing doesn't make them hard to read.

    Examples: different widths and spacing

    Bookman Old Style
    Arial Narrow

- *Expand your options by using "families."* A family includes a basic font and several variations. For example, if you check PowerPoint's font options, you will find Arial, Arial Black, and Arial Narrow. They could be used together because they are part of the same family, with Arial Black having an extremely heavy, extended appearance, which might make it useful if you were putting one big word on a photo-graph, and Arial Narrow using slim, tightly spaced letters, which might enable it to fit into small spaces.

- *Create the right impression.* Arial is one of the most common sans serif choices; Times New Roman is a top choice among serif fonts. Both are very legible. However, if you wanted a fresh, atypical look, then neither of these options would create that impression.

Make lettering large enough to be seen.   Fonts are sized in points, with a 72-point font being an inch, a 36-point font being half an inch, and so on. PowerPoint allows you to choose from a list of point sizes, but you can also customize any size you want; for instance, you can change the "20" in the box that shows font size to "21" and hit the "Enter" key to make text just a bit larger.

Because of the variation among fonts, providing size guidelines for the words and numbers on your visuals is difficult. Nevertheless, we will suggest some possibilities. If a font has a small x-height, start at the higher end of the range; if it has a large x-height, try the smaller options first.

- *For projection*: The distance between the projector and the screen will greatly affect the size of your words and numbers. If you can't test your font sizes with the projector and screen you will be using, then start with these parameters: (1) make your titles larger than other text, but small enough to work with your longest message title, somewhere between 28 and 40 point; (2) make the text used in bullet lists clearly smaller than the title, but large enough to be seen— perhaps 20 to 30 point for the main text and smaller for secondary text such as diagram labels; (3) be sure the text for chart numbers or sources is visible—perhaps 14 to 18 point.

- *For decks:* Use font sizes that are large enough for audience members to glance down and easily read the deck when it is placed on a table. You might try 18- to 24-point titles and 14- to 18-point text. Be careful with the small lettering used for labels or sources; older eyes may have trouble seeing tiny 8-, 9-, and even some 10-point fonts. If a deck is to be used more like a handout or distributed before your talk, then you can include more detail and smaller fonts since audience members won't be reading as you speak. In these cases, you might try 14- or 16-point titles and 11- or 12-point text.

- *For handouts based on your slides:* If your slides are simply designed, then the words on your handouts should be visible if you print two slide images per page. However, realize that 16-point text on your slide will only be 8 point in this format.

Enhance readability.   PowerPoint tempts you with many ways to alter and format text. These choices will influence the readability of your slides and deck pages and you should make them while you are designing the Slide Master.

- *Choose simple style options.* Wise choices for titles include plain text or bold. Avoid mixing several styles together (for example, a bold, italicized, shadow effect), which results in "letter junk." On the Slide Master, make the title bold if there isn't a clear variation between your title and text size. Do not, however, make the bullet text bold because that will make your slides and deck pages look too heavy and fail to make anything stand out.

- *Avoid all capital letters.* GRAPHIC DESIGN PROFESSOR LISA GRAHAM OFFERS THIS DOCUMENT DESIGN ADVICE: "AVOID ALL CAPS LIKE THE PLAGUE." LONG LINES OF CAPITALIZED TEXT ARE HARD TO READ AND CAN BE INTERPRETTED AS "SHOUTING" AT YOUR AUDIENCE, SO DON'T USE ALL CAPS AS PART OF YOUR MASTER.

- *Select an alignment for your titles.* Left justification is frequently the best alignment for your titles. However, if all your message titles are short, you might decide to center them. Centering creates a more formal impression, but it looks much better with charts and diagrams than it does with bullet lists. In addition, when titles wrap to a second line, centering them often looks odd; left justification tends to looks better and it enhances readability.

- *Test the line spacing.* If you plan to use text that will wrap to a second line, then test the line spacing. If text lines look too close together, go to "Line Spacing Options" and select the exact spacing you want. Base your choice on the font's point size and its x-height. For small to medium text fonts with an average x-height, try making the spacing 2- to 4-points larger than the text. If you have selected a medium font with a large x-height (for example, Verdana), then you will need to increase the line spacing even more.

- *Check the "Paragraph Spacing."* Although you won't be writing paragraphs, also adjust what's called the "Paragraph Spacing." It's the space that is inserted when you hit the "Enter" key, such as the space between bulleted items on a list. You want the space that separates two bullets to look larger than the space between two lines of text within a bullet.

- *Use simple, filled bullets.* Choose simple, filled bullets (such as • or ♦) making sure they are large enough to be seen, but not overpowering. Avoid fancy options (such as ➤ or ▣), which draw too much attention to themselves. When choosing a color for your bullet character, either match the text color or choose a subtle one. If you need second-level bullets, use a dash or small dot. Delete third-, fourth-, and fifth-level bullets, so you won't be tempted to use them.

3. Choosing simple backgrounds and layouts

Creating visuals with a unified, simple look requires some planning and lots of restraint. Whatever you add to your design will make your job more complex. When you design the Slide Master, you will be using various PowerPoint tools to help you position words and images in a consistent way. These tools work fairly well for slides, but they were not intended for decks; therefore, we suggest a few ways to deal with deck design issues. The last master you prepare will be the "Title Master" for the title slide or the deck's cover. If well designed, it will help unify your visuals.

Choosing a solid background: A solid background is the safest choice. Adding color variations may make a background look more interesting, but it will also affect the visibility of some text and require you to understand how to work with light and shadows. The worst background mistakes involve adding detailed images across a large portion of a slide. Such images limit the space you can use and add a needless distraction. Designer Nancy Duarte suggests that you think of your background like a canvas—a surface to hold all the content you will place on it. She thinks backgrounds should be "open, spacious, and simple." If you opt to alter your canvas, do so for a reason:

- *Inserting a line to emphasize a title:* To separate the title from the other text, you can draw a line under it. This addition helps if your title and text are the same color or a little too similar in size. When you select a line color, choose something visible, yet subtle.

- *Adding an edge to a black slide:* A black slide will seem to float on the screen. If you insert a design element, you can help people enclose the space around the slide. For instance, you could add a narrow band of color across the top. This stripe would anchor the slide and prevent it from blending with the screen.

- *Including a logo:* Make sure your background looks good with the logo or find out if it is acceptable to use either a "reverse image" (for example, a logo shown in all white rather than black) or a "grayscale" version of the logo, which is a color image transformed to black, grays, and white. Avoid plopping a logo with a white background on a colored slide; ask for a transparent background instead. Some logos take up lots of room, so think before you decide to include them on your master. You may want to use a logo only on some slides or pages.

Modifying placeholders: Placeholders confine text or images within a specific area. If you add background designs, you may need to move the title and text placeholders to accommodate the changes. For example, if you added a band of color to the top of your black slide, then you may need to move the title down and decrease the height of the text placeholder. The following image shows the various placeholders on the master: ❶ a title placeholder, ❷ a text placeholder, ❸ a date placeholder, ❹ a footer placeholder, and ❺ a page number placeholder. When you make changes to a placeholder on the master, those changes affect the corresponding placeholders on your other slides or pages. You probably won't use all these placeholders as you design. For example, you need page numbers on a deck, but you may not want them on your slides.

Positioning design elements on the Slide Master: PowerPoint also includes tools to help you position placeholders and graphics. The "Rulers" appear above and to the side of the slide; they help you locate the slide's center and gauge the space between objects. The "Grid" is meant to be a crude approximation of a tool used by professional designers. These dotted lines make it easier to align and place objects on slides. The "Slide Layouts" arrange the placeholders in various ways; some allow text or charts to extend across most of the screen, while others divide this space in half. If you make changes to placeholders, make sure they are used consistently throughout your slide show or deck.

Modifying the "Slide Master" for a deck: Decks are prone to more design errors than slides for many reasons. (1) They can hold more content than slides, so many presenters put far too much on each page. (2) The PowerPoint "Slide Master" is sized like a slide, not a deck page. (3) The prepared layouts were created for slides using large fonts; smaller fonts are very hard to read when they are formatted the same way. For these reasons and others, it takes more work to design a good master for a deck page.

- *Remember the invisible margin.* When you print your deck, a half-inch margin, not visible on the screen, will be added around the page.

- *Consider adjusting the margins.* Using larger margins may improve the look of your deck, especially since part of the top margin may be used for the spiral binding; however, don't just add space to the top. The bottom margin should be noticeably larger than the top one to prevent text and images from looking as if they are sliding down the page.

- *Modify the Slide Master (simple option).* Decrease the width of title and text placeholders so they don't extend across more than two-thirds to three-fourths of the screen. If a text placeholder allows you to create lines that use more than 10 words per line, then it is probably too wide for the font size. Either decrease the width of the placeholders or increase the size of the text. To maintain consistent layouts, keep charts and diagrams the same width as your text placeholder. Check "Print Preview" to see the invisible margins; make adjustments if needed.

- *Graph the layouts (advanced option).* Using standard-sized graph paper, mark the margins you want, then position the title and text placeholders. You might try dividing the page space into even columns and modifying the placeholders so they line up with the columns in various ways. Add design elements such as lines, logos, and page numbers, making sure they are used consistently on all layouts. Before transfering your layouts to PowerPoint masters, customize the Slide Master screen so it is 11" wide and 8.5"high.

Designing a title master: Although the title slide or deck cover will use a different layout than the other slides or pages, this image needs to coordinate with those that follow. For example, if you have used curved lines on your other layouts, use them on the title master as well; if not, don't put them there. Ideally, you want to feature your spot color somewhere on this slide or page. Also think about the other content you need to put on the title visual and arrange the layout so you can group items that belong together.

TIPS FOR DESIGNING A TEMPLATE

Getting started	Find the Master View. Use a plain, simple background and skip prepared PowerPoint templates and Design Themes.
Choosing colors	Use the "Custom Color Screen" to choose colors that (1) are appropriate for the audience, (2) provide contrast between the background and content, (3) include a spot color and dimming options.
Limiting colors	Avoid the "fruit salad effect" by limiting your scheme to three colors plus black, white, and gray. Use only one bold color as the spot color.
Selecting fonts	Choose one or two legible fonts: (1) one font in various sizes for titles, text, labels, and so on; (2) one font plus a variation from the same "family"; (3) two complementary fonts.
Sizing fonts	In addition to point size, remember that x-height and the thickness and shape of letters influence how large the font will look. Use the following ranges to test visibility. *For slides:* *For decks:* Titles from 28- to 40-point Titles about 18- to 24-point Main text from 20- to Main text about 14- to 30-point 18-point
Formatting titles and text	Use simple styles. Bold is good for titles, but don't use it on all text. Avoid PowerPoint temptations, ranging from shadow text to Word Art.
Customizing the line spacing	Test spacing between text lines. Use the "Paragraph Spacing" screen to increase line spacing; add even more space between the bullet points.
Adding graphics to the master	Add graphics for a reason. Use the rulers and the grid lines to position them.
Modifying placeholders	Delete placeholders you don't need. If altering a placeholder, check the effect on others.

4. Using company templates

Having a great company-mandated template may make your job much easier because someone has already chosen the colors, fonts, and layouts that match your needs. In reality, however, you may not be quite so lucky: you may have a company template you have been struggling with for years or face a one-time challenge from a template created for a conference or special event. In our experience, these problems are widespread and can be linked to a variety of issues, ranging from logo challenges to busy background designs.

If you have identified template issues, explain them to other people in the organization. Perhaps together you will find a creative way to fix the problem and maintain the guidelines.

Logo challenges: Logos help shape an organization's identity, so it makes sense that many organizations want to feature them on slide shows and decks. However, sometimes logos pose problems.

- *Large or colorful logos:* Simple logos are the easiest to use. Large, colorful ones pose the greatest challenges. Ask if you can make a logo less noticeable by making it smaller or changing its color. As another alternative, find out whether it's permissible to omit the logo from slides that use charts, diagrams, and photographs.

- *Logos that interfere with titles:* Sometimes logos and titles are placed together, perhaps within a colored band at the top of the slide. On such templates, long titles can get too close to the logo. To separate them, try making the title a little smaller, using very brief message titles, or wrapping titles at a logical point so they remain in the upper left corner, far away from the logo. If the logo is to the left of the title, ask if you can flip the placement. If not, try using right justification for the title.

Title troubles: You will have to make compromises if you see titles formatted in all capital letters; right-justified titles; or deck titles used as summaries, placed at the bottom of the page.

- *Titles formatted in all capital letters:* Most designers agree that long lines of text shouldn't be in all caps, so if they appear on your deck template, the designer probably expected your title to be a word or brief phrase. Although not ideal, you can compromise by using a single-word title in all capital letters and adding a message title below it.

- *Right-justified titles:* If the template uses this format, try to avoid wrapping any titles. If they must wrap, keep the lines as even as possible, perhaps editing your titles until you find a message that will logically divide in half.

- *Deck titles used as page summaries:* Some deck templates place summary titles at the bottom. If you can shorten these summaries, do so. If not, write them in two parts, using a bold heading to capture a brief message, followed by regularly formatted text to add the required details. You might also be able to add an attention-getting graphic to the bottom of the page.

Color issues: Some color schemes are too restrictive, while others include colors you may not want to use.

- *Too few colors:* If a slide template uses only one color plus black, gray, and white, you won't risk falling prey to the fruit salad effect, but you may have trouble highlighting important points on your slide. Using lighter or darker variations of the color might give the flexibility you need. If the lone color has been used for the background, consider including another one, perhaps a color you have seen used in corporate brochures. Even if this color isn't especially vivid, it will still stand out as a spot color in a limited color scheme.

- *Colors you don't want to include:* If you don't like some of the colors in the palette avoid using them by relying instead on black, white, and gray, and the one color you do like for emphasis.

Background woes: The two most common background problems are (1) intense background colors that are not light or dark and (2) designs that take up too much of the screen or page.

- *Intense slide backgrounds:* We have seen templates that use very intense mid-range blues, greens, and purples. Thankfully, most of them relied on white text since many other options would be difficult to see. Inserting a line under the title can help distinguish a white title and white text. Adding a white or black rectangle behind your charts and diagrams might also be necessary.

- *Busy background designs:* If a design takes up more than 20 percent of your slide or page, it isn't going to work with most charts and diagrams. You may be able to use the background design with text slides and pages, but ask if another layout—a very simple one—can be created. You might also try using a plain background that matches the color underneath the template design.

III. THINK VISUALLY AS YOU DESIGN.

Once you have a well-designed template, focus on the content you will put on each slide or page. Use charts, diagrams, photographs, and other options, so your visual aids are actually visual.

1. Data-driven charts explain the numbers.

Every table of numbers offers scores of potential messages. It's your job to locate these messages, decide which ones are relevant, and turn the corresponding numbers into accurate and easy-to-comprehend charts. To do so, follow Gene Zelazny's method: (1) determine your message; (2) identify the comparison; and (3) select the chart form. Using this approach, we'll examine four data comparisons.

Time series (changes over time):   With this comparison, time is plotted on the x-axis. The change can be measured in seconds, days, or even decades; the message can focus on increases, steady growth, or an unexpected decline. If your message is about a pattern occurring over time, then you have three options: column, line, or area charts.

- *Choose column charts for limited data points* and for times when you want to emphasize specific numbers as much as the trend. To make your column chart more visual, increase the width of the columns and reduce the space between them. Delete details that distract from your message, as explained on page 116.

- *Use line charts to emphasize trends.* When you have many data points, a line chart will show the trend more elegantly than columns. Unfortunately, PowerPoint doesn't make very effective line charts. To improve their look, set the trend line to at least a 4-point width and use a visible color. Save dotted lines for times when you are forecasting trends. Always eliminate the "chartjunk" as shown on page 115. And don't use more than three trend lines, or you may end up with a tangled mess, which Zelazny has dubbed "a spaghetti chart."

- *Be careful with area charts.* Because an area chart colors the space under the trend line, this chart looks more dramatic than a line chart. However, don't use area charts to show more than a single trend or the resulting stacks will confuse viewers.

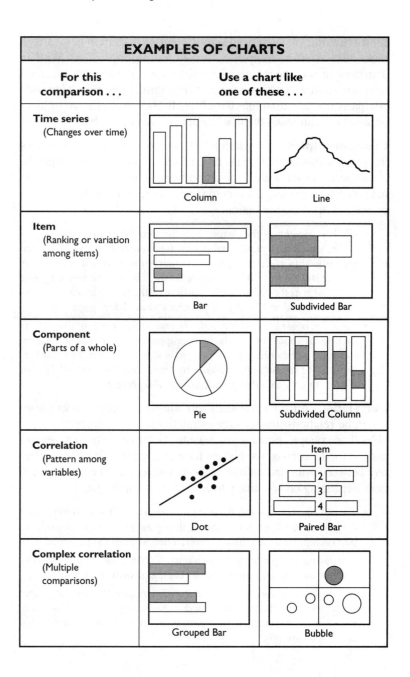

EXAMPLES OF CHARTS	
For this comparison . . .	**Use a chart like one of these . . .**
Time series (Changes over time)	Column Line
Item (Ranking or variation among items)	Bar Subdivided Bar
Component (Parts of a whole)	Pie Subdivided Column
Correlation (Pattern among variables)	Dot Paired Bar
Complex correlation (Multiple comparisons)	Grouped Bar Bubble

Item (ranking or variation among items):   An item comparison ranks items, such as companies, survey results, or products. With an item comparison, the message isn't about time. It's about how certain items are similar or which one ranks first, third, or even last. For such comparisons, use a simple bar chart. Bar charts are easy to label because you can insert the label beside or even on the bar.

Component (parts of a whole):   A component comparison shows the relationship among parts of a whole. Your message might be about percentages, shares, or proportions. For components of one item, choose a pie chart; for components of multiple items, you will probably select another option.

- *Choose pie charts for simple comparisons.* Pie charts are easy to make, which may explain why they are sometimes overused. If you are projecting a pie chart, limit the number of slices; more than six will be difficult to differentiate and label. If you are featuring one slice, put it at the "12 o'clock" position of the pie. In all cases, eliminate the legend and label your pie slices as we did on page 115.

- *Consider other choices for multiple component comparisons.* If the message is about how one budget component changes over time, then use subdivided columns, with a y-axis that goes from 0 to 100 percent. If the message isn't linked to time, then consider subdivided bars, with an x-axis that goes from 0 to 100 percent.

Correlation (pattern between variables):   These comparisons show the relationship—or lack of relationship—between two variables. For example, perhaps you want to show that the most expensive canned foods received the highest taste-test ratings. To show the pattern between price and ratings, you could choose a dot chart or paired bars, depending on how many food items were in the data pool.

- *Try dot charts when you have many data points.* If you were plotting the price and ratings for 20 items, then your best option would be to plot each point with a dot and insert a line to show the pattern.

- *Use paired bars for limited data points.* If comparing the price and ratings for four items, then use paired bars, as shown on page 101.

- *Be careful with complex correlation comparisons.* Be especially careful with bubble charts, which are dot charts with an extra dimension: the size of the dot. These charts need to be built gradually and explained carefully.

2. Concept diagrams depict ideas.

While data-driven charts help people understand your quantitative messages, concept diagrams enable them to picture your qualitative ideas. Lines, shapes, and your imagination are the building blocks of diagrams. You can easily find examples that illustrate relationships or indicate sequence. With a little more effort, you can also find ways to communicate less common ideas.

Some diagrams illustrate relationships.   On page 104, you will find examples of diagrams that show how items or ideas interact, how they are structured, and how they compare.

- *To show interaction:* You can use overlapping circles (known as a Venn diagram) to show the intersection of two or more ideas. Or, you can show that ideas are connected by placing them along a shape's perimeter and inserted dotted lines or arrows, as we did with the AIM triangle on page 2. You can also combine arrows and shapes to depict how some items are influencing others.

- *To emphasize structure*: Organizational charts and idea charts show how people, positions, or ideas are linked. A pyramid diagram, which is shown on page 104, emphasizes the foundation of a structure. If items are organized around a hub or core idea, then a honeycomb pattern, or something similar, can communicate that point.

- *To compare concepts:* A T-chart can be used to separate items so they can be viewed side by side. For more complex interactions, consider a matrix, which divides space into quadrants.

Other diagrams highlight sequence.   They can show the steps in a process, the order of events, or the repetition of stages.

- *To indicate linear flow:* Arrows, chevrons, and lines can show movement. A chevron is a good way to highlight the stages of a project. A series of shapes linked by a line or arrows will also communicate linear flow.

- *To show time sequence:* Time lines can illustrate events over time. Gantt charts are a type of time line; they position bars over a time line to show the starting and stopping points for stages of a project.

- *To depict circular flow:* When flow isn't linear, use curved arrows to show how stages repeat. Linking shapes with curved arrows or a circle can also depict this flow.

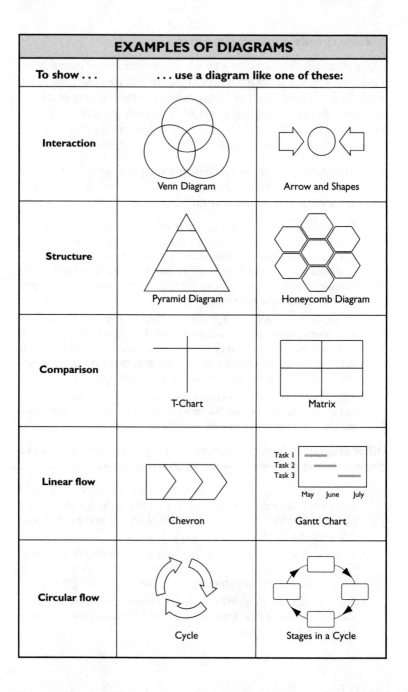

EXAMPLES OF DIAGRAMS		
To show . . .	**. . . use a diagram like one of these:**	
Interaction	Venn Diagram	Arrow and Shapes
Structure	Pyramid Diagram	Honeycomb Diagram
Comparison	T-Chart	Matrix
Linear flow	Chevron	Gantt Chart
Circular flow	Cycle	Stages in a Cycle

Uncommon diagrams stand out.   A chevron is common. Its familiarity makes its meaning easy to grasp. However, common diagrams also have drawbacks: they aren't as interesting as a novel approach and they may not work for your message. For instance, you need an atypical diagram to show that a big change is pulling others behind it.

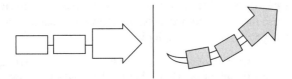

Find inspiration from many sources.   For people who have trouble visualizing concepts as diagrams, PowerPoint added a feature called "SmartArt." Because we are willing to bet that you are smarter than this art, we recommend you look for diagram ideas outside PowerPoint. Books such as *Say It with Charts* and *slide:ology* (cited in the bibliography) offer dozens of ideas. If you look at them and start to doodle, you will come up with new possibilities. If, however, you do use SmartArt, you can "Ungroup" a prepared diagram to delete parts you don't want; you can even delete the labels and use a "Text Box" to make and position labels instead.

Match the diagram to your message.   Don't just select the first diagram you see and squeeze your ideas into it.

- *Consider what the diagram means.* For example, save chevrons for items that flow from one to the next, choose a Venn diagram only when items actually overlap, and use circular flows only when the last item leads back to the first.
- *Make shapes bigger, bolder, or central for a reason.* If you are showing a core idea, then position it in the middle or where the audience will look first. If items are similar, then make them appear that way.
- *Check the arrows.* Think what an arrow communicates and resist the urge to use too many of them, unless your message is about chaos or confusion. Downward arrows suggest a somewhat negative message. Curved and diagonal arrows imply more movement and excitement than straight ones; save them for messages about energy, change, cycles, or tension.

3. Photographs add interest.

Photographs can be a wonderful addition to your slide show or deck, but too often they are inserted without enough thought. If a picture is worth 1,000 words, then a bad picture is really worth avoiding. Therefore, only choose images that clarify your message and look good with the other items on the slide or page.

Finding pictures: Many photos are protected by copyright and you can't use them without permission. However, usable pictures are available if you know where to look.

- *Inserting Microsoft images:* Some of the photos in PowerPoint's clip art selection might be useful, but the best ones may have already been seen since these images are so easy to access.

- *Finding free photos:* Some images are in the "public domain," and you may be able to use them, even for company presentations. In general, these images were created by government employees as part of their jobs or they are old and no longer copyright protected. (For more details about copyright and tips on how to find public domain photos, see www.publicdomainsherpa.com.) A few sites are dedicated to making free images available; www.morguefile.com not only offers free photos, but also links to other sites with free images.

- *Purchasing images:* You can buy photos from reasonably priced sources, such as www.dreamstime.com or www.istockphoto.com. You can also purchase CD or DVD collections, which often focus on one theme. Read the terms before you buy. Like free photos, purchased ones may have some limits as to how they can be used.

- *Supplying your own images:* If you have your own digital camera and are skilled using it, then you may be able to capture an image that communicates your message.

Choosing images: Be selective. The audience should never wonder why you have included a photo so pick one that clearly conveys your point. For example, bypass images that look silly or staged, unless you are sending a campy message. When possible, choose a photo that matches your color scheme. Examine the picture's shape and consider how it will look with the other content on the slide or page. Always test the clarity of any image you choose; see how it projects on a screen or prints on a deck page. Sometimes a blurry photo can be usable if you make it smaller.

Altering photos: If necessary, alter a picture so it looks better on your slide or page. You can resize a photo, but always keep the proportions the same so you don't stretch or squish the image. If the colors aren't right, switch to grayscale or use picture editing software to adjust them. As noted in the following table, you can also crop a photo to change its shape or focal point. In the 2007 version of PowerPoint, you can even turn a square photo into a round one.

Positioning photos: Pictures grab attention so position them carefully. With slide shows, filling the whole screen with a photo can be very powerful; place it on a black background so nothing but the image projects on the screen. When grouping photos, arrange them so they look balanced; align their edges or create a montage with a primary focus (one picture that stands out because of its color, size, or shape). As shown below, also make sure any photo you include guides a viewer's eyes in the right direction.

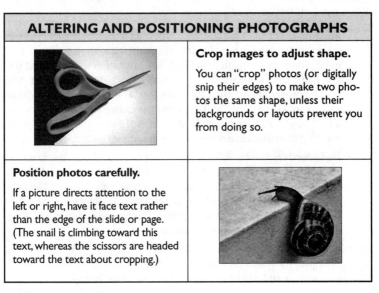

ALTERING AND POSITIONING PHOTOGRAPHS

	Crop images to adjust shape. You can "crop" photos (or digitally snip their edges) to make two photos the same shape, unless their backgrounds or layouts prevent you from doing so.
Position photos carefully. If a picture directs attention to the left or right, have it face text rather than the edge of the slide or page. (The snail is climbing toward this text, whereas the scissors are headed toward the text about cropping.)	

Photos: morguefile.com (J. Sawyer and L. Solonynko)

Capturing interest with other options: There are many other ways to add visual interest. You can include drawings, ranging from an image supplied by an artist to a simple one you add yourself. Using maps is another option; they can show where a global corporation has opened offices or how to find a local restaurant. If they are appropriate, cartoons can add a bit of humor. With slides, you can add motion and sound by using video clips.

4. Animation clarifies complex slides.

"Animation" is the PowerPoint tool that allows you to build—or systematically reveal—one point or image at time. By using animation, you control the flow of information, which will prevent audience members from becoming confused or reading ahead. Avoid the temptation to create flashing arrows, flying bullets, or pointless motion between slides. Instead, select simple options such as "Appear" or one that focuses attention on your point and not the movement on the screen.

- *Build lines of text.* Your audience will read ahead. However, you can use animation and dimmed text to focus their attention on the current point. For example, with bullet lists, use animation when the text line acts like a topic sentence, listing a point you plan to talk about in great detail; however, don't use it for quick lists where you won't be adding content to what's on the slide. As another example, you should virtually always build your agenda slide; it will force you to slow down and help your audience focus on your important points.

- *Build complex charts.* Adding animation can help the audience understand your point. For example, with a bubble chart, you might begin with the title and axes, making sure the comparisons are clear. Next you might add the featured bubble and discuss its placement and size. Finally, you could add other bubbles, perhaps a quadrant at a time, pointing out what you want the audience to see.

- *Add layers to diagrams.* If a diagram is complex, then build it. For example, show the foundation of a pyramid diagram, then dim the base's color and add new layers, until you reach the top.

- *Avoid distracting transitions.* "Transitions" are the movement from one slide to the next. Spinning wheels and dissolving checkerboards are a distraction as are transitions that include silly sounds. Unless you are adding movement to emphasize your message, it's usually better to let slides simply appear on the screen.

5. Text charts list important details.

Although not especially visual, bullet lists do have a role; they distinguish a main message—the title—from less important details. Other types of text visuals document quotes and, in the case of a deck, provide summaries. When you use visuals that rely on words, do your best to (1) keep them simple, (2) use parallel structure, (3) fine-tune the formatting, and (4) add a visual flourish.

Keep slides exceptionally simple.   A great debate rages about how many words should be on a slide. Some experts advocate for fewer than six words per bullet; others opt for the less extreme view of no more than two lines per bullet. Yet all of them agree that filling a slide with words is a terrible idea.

In a medium-sized font, it takes about six lines of text averaging six words per line to go halfway down and across a slide. Once you reach this "6 × 6" point, you should be worried about the audience's reaction. Some people won't mind; others will be more irritated with your visuals than interested in your comments.

How many words are too many?

- The six-word title is Calibri.
- The text uses the same font.
- Calibri's small "x-height" means you would choose one of the larger text sizes, such as 30-point text.
- Even so, about 10 words would fit on the longer lines of text, making them a bit difficult to read.
- Once the 7th line of text is added, this slide looks extremely overloaded.
- If we remind you to adjust the line spacing and to avoid long bullets that wrap to a 3rd line, then we just made a truly bad slide even worse.

Keep deck pages simple.   You can put more words on a deck page than a slide, but the more you use, the harder it will be to keep your presentation from turning into a group reading session. Decks viewed during a presentation should feature images rather than words.

To keep your text visuals simple, consider the following suggestions:

- *Use telegram language.* Look ~~out~~ for ~~all those~~ extra words ~~that aren't needed~~. To pare the wording on your visuals, use what visual aids expert Charlotte Rosen calls "telegram language"—words that create a clear message, without the extra letters that would make a telegram expensive to send:

Wordy phrase	*Brief "telegram" language*
in order to	to
each and every member	members
continue to advocate for	push for

- *Maintain stand-alone sense.* Although you want to simplify bullet lists, you don't want to cut so much that they no longer make stand-alone sense as explained on page 83.

Lacks stand-alone sense	*Makes stand-alone sense*
• Jobs	• High-paying, local jobs
• Energy	• Carbon-free, safe energy
• Subsidies	• Long-term, federal subsidies

- *Switch to active voice:* Active voice relies on strong verbs such as "decide," "use," and "create," while passive voice softens the tone, using weaker verbs such as "is," "there are," and "might be." Often passive voice uses more words. For example, assume a title reads, "Additional learning will result from the continued use of behavior scan testing." Switched to active voice, this title claims, "Behavior scan testing assists our research." You might be able to cut lots of words on your deck pages by using more active voice. To learn more, download the plain language handbook provided by the Security and Exchange Commission: www.sec.gov/pdf/handbook.pdf.

- *Limit your use of subpoints:* Don't create subpoints for your subpoints. Once a bullet list looks more like an outline than a list, it loses even more visual appeal.

Use parallel structure.   To be clear and consistent, lists need to use parallel structure—which includes both grammatical and conceptual parallelism. The audience will have a much easier time understanding your ideas if they are listed with the same grammatical construction and in a way that distinguishes main and subordinate points.

- *Grammatical parallelism:* If the first words of all the items on your list use the same part of speech (for example, all nouns or all action verbs), then your job will also be easier; you are less likely to stumble when you transition from one point to the next if each line of text begins the same way.

Not grammatically parallel	*Grammatically parallel*
• Checking health-care plans	• Check health-care plans
• Comparison of dental plans	• Compare dental plans
• About pension funds	• Review pension funds

- *Conceptual parallelism:* Sometimes the main idea gets combined with lesser points and the real title for your slide isn't in bold letters at the top; instead, you find it tucked away at the bottom of a list. Or maybe some of the points in your list don't seem to match the title. Professor Joann Yates coined the term "conceptual parallelism" to refer to times when subpoints and main points don't go together. In the following example, the problem becomes clear as soon as you realize pension funds don't have anything to do with health care:

Not conceptually parallel	*Conceptually parallel*
Learn about health care	**Learn about your benefits**
• Check health-care plans	• Check health and dental plans
• Compare dental plans	• Review pension funds
• Review pension funds	

Fine-tune the formatting. Before you start adding text, turn off the features that automatically downsize title and text fonts to make them fit in their placeholders: (1) In older versions of PowerPoint, these features are in the "Tools" menu. (2) In the 2007 version, you need to click on the "office button" in the upper left corner of the screen. At the bottom of the menu, you will find "PowerPoint Options." From there, click on "Proofing," and then "Autocorrect Options." Make sure the "Autofit Title Text to Placeholder" and "Autofit Body Text to Placeholder" choices are not checked.

Once you are ready to insert text, you have formatting choices to make, in addition to those you made for the Slide Master. Think about how you will use capital letters, break long lines of text, and highlight important information.

- *Consider your use of case.* For titles, you have two options. You can use title case, which capitalizes the first letter of each word. Or you can use sentence case, which only capitalizes the first letter of the first word. If you centered your titles, then title case tends to look better. With left-justified titles, we often prefer sentence case. For bullet lists, chose either sentence case or lower case; title case will make your text lines much harder to read. If you plan to use lower case, then turn off the autocorrect feature that capitalizes the first word in a line of text.

- *Wrap lines of text so they look balanced.* Try not to leave a single word by itself on a line. Instead, divide the title or text line in a way that makes sense, based on the content. If the right margin of a long quote looks uneven, try to even it by breaking lines of text. To do so, position the curser where you want the line to end, then hold down the "Shift" and "Enter" keys.

- *Use simple highlighting options.* If you decide to highlight a word or line, do so with care. Too much boldface text will make nothing stand out; italics will look less dramatic, but will be hard to read if used for large blocks of text. Placing words vertically or curving them with "Word Art" won't help readability either. Finally, save all capital letters for labels or single words, using them SPARINGLY.

Add a visual flourish.   Some people disguise their bullet lists by enclosing each point in a shape or putting the whole list in a box. You can also put a photograph next to a list, as long as the image directs attention toward the text. The following slide images show how a list can become a bit more visual.

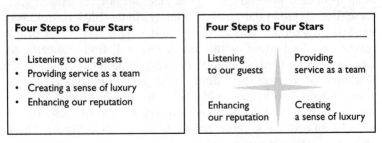

IV. EDIT YOUR EFFORTS.

Make sure your visuals have a clear structure, use color and graphics effectively, and print or project without errors.

I. Verify that the structure is clear.

To check the structure, focus on your preview visual. In a slide show, you may want to repeat this slide between each section of your talk. In a deck, you might want to include section visuals that are linked to the table of contents. In complex slide shows or decks, you might also want to insert trackers to reinforce the structure.

Repeating the preview slide: Copy and insert the preview slide before each section, highlighting the section that comes next.

Examples of highlighted preview visuals

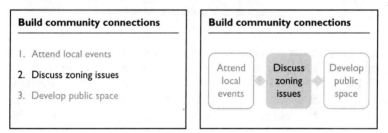

Adding trackers: A tracker is a word or symbol that links a visual to the correct section. Make trackers small, but visible.

Tracker examples: word lower right and symbols at bottom

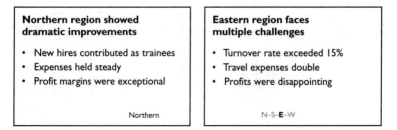

2. Enhance the visual effect.

In addition to editing for structure, check the visual effect of your colors and graphics.

Check your use of color.   Look at your diagrams and charts to make sure they are using spot and dimming colors to emphasize the title. The following examples show how color can detract from a diagram's message or enhance the visual effect.

Overuse of color   *Good use of spot color*

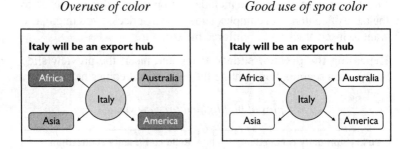

Use graphics as a "pointer."   You can add arrows, lines, circles, or boxes to highlight something on a page. As previously noted, with slides you can also use animation to control the flow of information. Graphics can appear with the slide or they can be added with a click of your mouse; either way, they will guide people's eyes to just the right spot.

Using an arrow or a shape to direct attention

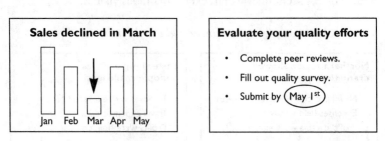

Eliminate chartjunk. To use the term coined by design expert Edward Tufte, eliminate "chartjunk"—those extra design elements that don't contribute to your message. The following examples show how clutter can detract from a pie, bar, and line chart. The table on page 116 lists specific PowerPoint problems (such as legends used to indicate the color coding of pie slices, bar segments, or trend lines) that you will want to overcome.

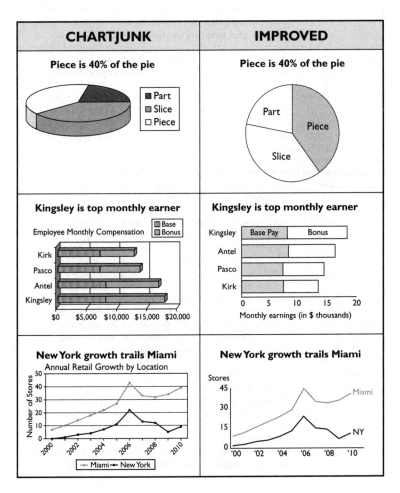

ELIMINATING CHARTJUNK IN POWERPOINT

Challange	Solution
Avoiding 3D	3D distorts the data so select the 2D views.
Deleting legends	Legends slow down the viewer. Cut them from pie, line, and bar charts (and complex column charts if possible). In 2007 version, use legend button on chart layout ribbon to choose "none." In earlier versions, click twice on the legend after it is already in the chart, then right click to delete it.
Labeling chart elements	Use the "text box" to make labels. Position them with arrow keys and "align" tools. Place labels on or near pie slices, next to or on bars, and near lines.
Simplifying titles and labels	Delete repetitive titles. Eliminate extra zeros by adding "thousands" or "millions" to axis label instead. When data points are clearly labeled (for example, "May," "June," "July"), cut needless axis labels such as "Months."
Avoiding vertical column labels	Avoid vertical and angled labels under columns by making columns wider, not using too many columns, and using brief labels ("5/12" for "May 2012").
Changing width of columns/bars	To increase their default width, edit the "data series," using the option that lets you make the "gap width" smaller.
Improving line charts	Click on the line chart, then right click on the trend line and go to "format data series," where you can choose the line's color, increase its width, and cut "data markers"—the little squares, triangles, or circles that appear on the trend line.
Cutting borders and extra lines	Eliminate the border or background that appears around the chart. Cut grid lines not needed to clarify meaning; delete small lines or "tick marks" jutting out from each axis.
Adjusting chart colors	Click on the pie chart; then click on a pie slice. Next, right click on the pie slice to recolor it. Use spot color for key slice and dimming option for less important ones. Recolor lines, bars, and columns the same way.
Positioning slices and bars	Insert data in an order that makes sense based on the message. Make the key pie slice appear at 12 o'clock position; make sure bars are arranged in a logical way.

3. Proof and proof again.

The last refinements involve checking for consistency and correctness. You want to maintain consistent phrasing, document your sources, and confirm that your slides and pages are error-free.

Maintain consistent phrasing.   Use the same wording on your slides and pages that you did on your preview visual. For example, if you list "financial projections" on your preview slide, don't switch to "spreadsheet analysis" on the supporting visual. Similarly, if using trackers, link them to your preview. For instance, if you wrote "Northern Region" in the table of contents and used the word "Northern" as a tracker, the connection would be clear. However, if "Mid-Atlantic Region" was listed in the preview, with the word "Eastern" used as its tracker, the connection wouldn't be so obvious.

Document your sources.   If you are using a chart, cite any numbers that come from outside the organization. If you don't know the source, then you shouldn't be using the data. Similarly, if you use an expert's words, identify them as that person's ideas and not your own. On projected visuals, use limited citations, perhaps just noting the publication or the author's last name. On decks, you can include more detail. You might even want to include a bibliography in the appendix.

Check for errors.   One of the easiest ways to allow little mistakes to creep into your visuals is to proof them, make last-minute changes, and fail to proof them again.

- *Don't rely on the spell-checker:* Lots of mistakes get caught with this tool, but many others are missed. If you are not a detail person, then ask someone to check your slides or pages. Print your work; it's easier to find errors on a printed page than on your computer screen.

- *Check the numbers one more time.* It can be a real credibility killer for someone to spot a mistake on your chart so double-check the numbers and make sure you didn't transpose any digits when you entered the data. In a deck, there is another set of numbers that is essential to check: page numbers. Make sure your table of contents matches the actual pages and there isn't a page missing in anyone's deck.

- *Test the animation and colors in a slide show.* Run through the slide show and make sure items appear the way you intended. As soon as possible, test your colors on the big screen.

CHAPTER 6 OUTLINE

  I. ANALYZE YOUR NONVERBAL STYLE.
- 1. Body position and movement
- 2. Hand and arm gestures
- 3. Eye contact and facial expression
- 4. Vocal traits
- 5. Space and objects around you

  II. PRACTICE YOUR NONVERBAL DELIVERY.
- 1. Check your content and timing.
- 2. Rehearse with your visuals.

  III. MANAGE YOUR NERVOUS SYMPTOMS.
- 1. General techniques
- 2. Physical techniques
- 3. Mental techniques
- 4. Last-minute tips

CHAPTER 6

Refine Your Nonverbal Delivery

The third part of implementation focuses on your nonverbal skills—how you look and sound to your audience. We all know that nonverbal elements are crucial to a presentation's success. Even so, "perfect" delivery is not necessary. In fact, it's not even possible since different people prefer different delivery styles.

Although you always want to look and sound natural, you will want to adapt your delivery to the formality of the situation. With practice, you should be able to develop a range of effective delivery behaviors that all look and sound like you. As you work on your delivery, use the suggestions in this chapter to (1) analyze your nonverbal style, (2) practice your nonverbal delivery, and (3) manage your nervous symptoms.

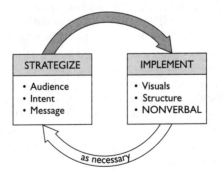

I. ANALYZE YOUR NONVERBAL STYLE.

Many nonverbal elements affect your delivery. Some are your own behaviors, such as your gesturing habits and facial expression. You can observe them by watching a recording of yourself or rehearsing in front of a mirror. Other nonverbal elements are separate from you, such as the lighting in the room and the distance between you and your audience. You will become more aware of these factors if you rehearse in the place where you will be presenting. All of these nonverbal behaviors are situational: they vary by personality, place, audience, and culture.

1. Body position and movement

How you position and move your body communicates a great deal. Do your best to look confident.

Distracting positions are often obvious from the start of a presentation. Where you position your legs and feet affects your whole body and influences how you move.

- *The informal "hip sit":* If you rest your weight on one leg or "park on your hip," your stance will look informal. The distractions begin when your legs get tired: if you switch back and forth, from one leg to the other, the unintended motion can attract unwanted attention.

- *Problematic foot placement:* Standing with your feet too far apart makes you look like a ranch hand doing the "cowpoke straddle." However, placing them too close together makes you look submissive. Be sure to check your toes: if they are pointed away from your heels, in a "duck stance," you may look as if you are waddling when you walk.

- *Leaning troubles:* Leaning positions such as the "podium clutch" and "table lean" leave your legs and feet free to do distracting things— such as swing, wrap, twist, or tap.

- *Moving mistakes:* Watch for distracting motion, such as bouncing, rocking, and pacing. Also avoid taking single steps up and back or side to side. Such, repetitive, purposeless motion distracts the audience.

- *Sloppy sitting:* Check how people sit around a conference table. Slouching doesn't look professional. Swiveling soon gets distracting.

Effective formal positions usually involve standing; being above your audience creates a more formal environment than being seated at the same level. Standing on a stage, behind a podium, creates an exceptionally formal look. But even when you are standing in front of a small group, you will want to use a solid opening stance and combine it with movement that is appropriate for the situation.

- *Position your legs and feet formally.* To create a formal opening stance: (1) place your feet about shoulder-width apart, rather than very close together or far apart; (2) distribute your weight evenly, using both legs equally for support; (3) divide your weight between your heels and the balls of your feet; (4) make sure your feet are straight and not in "duck" position; and (5) don't lock your knees. This position tends to feel awkward until you get used to it, but it looks good and prevents unintended movement.

- *Return to the formal stance after you move.* In formal situations, it's fine to move for a reason—to emphasize a point on your visual aid, for example, or to move closer to the audience to signal that you are seeking questions. Just make sure your feet are in the formal position described earlier once you have finished moving.

Effective informal positions include more options. For example, you can signal that you want to create an informal exchange by leaning momentarily against a table or using a more casual posture. You might also choose to present from a chair.

Environmental factors influence where you stand and how you move: (1) *Room size* is one consideration. For example, in a large room, one effective way to use movement is to walk to a new place in the room to indicate that you are beginning a new section of your talk. (2) *Seating arrangements* may also be a factor. For example, in a "U-shape" arrangement, you don't want to spend too much time in the center of the room since people on the side will only have a view of your back.

Personal style also affects movement. Some people have lots of energy and prefer to move around the room; they need to be careful not to walk too much and to remain still at times, giving the audience a break from all that motion. Other presenters prefer to stay in one place, sometimes seeking safety behind a podium; they may want to walk to a new place, when appropriate, to add variety to their delivery.

2. Hand and arm gestures

When standing, many presenters feel awkward: they don't know where to put their hands, and their arms suddenly feel too long. To use your hands and arms effectively, we suggest you (1) discover your natural gesturing style, (2) avoid distracting gestures, (3) use conversational patterns, and (4) adapt to the situation.

Discover your natural gesturing style.   To do so, get a sense of your gesturing habits in various situations, such as when you are talking at a cocktail party or across a dinner table. Ask people who know you to comment on how often you gesture and which gestures you tend to use. Inquire about the size of your gestures, and find out about any distracting arm, hand, or finger habits. Even better, arrange to be recorded so you can see an example of your gesturing style for yourself.

Avoid distracting gestures.   Once you learn about your tendencies, you will want to eliminate distracting gestures and avoid overusing your favorites. Some small, repetitive, gestures are signs of stress. These nervous fidgets include touching your hair, rubbing your face, and twisting your ring, just to describe a few. In addition, many hand and arm positions have descriptive or humorous names; they tend to send the wrong nonverbal message.

- *The commander* places her hands on her hips.
- *The chilly presenter* crosses his arms over his chest.
- *The gun-shot victim* clings to her upper arm with one hand.
- *The armless presenter* leaves his hands behind his back.
- *The pocket jingler* puts a hand in her pocket, shaking keys and coins.
- *The clutcher* grasps a pen or pointer and never puts the object down.
- *The slapper* makes noise as he hits his palms against his thighs.
- *The exposed presenter* clasps her hands in front of her, where a "figleaf" would be.

Use conversational patterns.   Aside from avoiding distracting gestures, you want your gesturing style as a speaker to match the style you use in conversations. If possible, you also want to use some gestures that reinforce your points.

- *Emphasize your message.* Some gestures go along with your verbal content, adding nonverbal reinforcement to your message. For example, if you are "balancing two issues," your palms might be turned up, alternately moving up and down to simulate a scale. Try not to force such gestures. The best emphatic gestures are those you really tend to use.

- *Avoid extremes.* Most of your gestures should be below your face and above your waist. Watch for extremes: if you use lots of huge gestures that extend down to your knees and over your head, you may look more like a cheerleader than a business presenter. On the other hand, if you keep your hands at your sides and use only tiny movements, you may resemble a flapping penguin.

- *Point appropriately.* Reserve pointing for visual aids, not for people. Or try "friendly pointing" that uses your whole hand, keeping your palm sidewise or tilted slightly up and your fingers together.

- *Refine, but don't obsess.* Remember, you don't need to be perfect. You might fidget once, slap your thigh, overuse your favorite gesture, and still accomplish your presentation objective. Practice to refine your gesturing style, but don't obsess about it.

Adapt to the situation.   Although you want them to be natural, your gestures should also be influenced by the environment and the expectations of the audience.

- *Consider room size.* In a large room, gestures can be big and still look appropriate; however, speaking in a small space or appearing on a TV screen requires smaller gestures.

- *Think about your audience.* Some people like presenters who gesture often. Others prefer limited gesturing. You can't please everyone, so usually it's best to use your own style. However, if you see that people are staring at your hands, perhaps you'll want to scale back some of your gesturing. Similarly, if you tend to look a bit too formal, adding a few gestures, especially friendly "palms up" gestures, can make your style seem less rigid.

- *Consider cultural norms.* In some cultures, expansive gestures are common, while in other cultures gesturing tends to be far more restrained. One of the most important cultural differences to consider involves hand signals that stand on their own. What you use to show "OK" may not mean "everything is all right" in some cultures. Similarly, the "thumbs up" and "stop" signals have various meanings. Be very careful when using such gestures in cross-cultural situations; you don't want to unintentionally send an insulting or even vulgar message.

3. Eye contact and facial expression

Your face plays a crucial role in your nonverbal delivery style: your eye contact connects you to your audience, and your face communicates interest, confidence, and enthusiasm.

Eye contact: Most U.S. business audiences want you to "look them in the eye"—a mark of honesty and confidence according to cultural norms. Here are some tips to assist you as you use eye contact to connect with your audience:

- *Find a friendly face.* If you are nervous, making eye contact with a supportive person might actually calm you down. The smiles and nods you see from the friendly face can help you get through the difficult parts of your presentation and boost your confidence.

- *Have little conversations.* Imagine you are speaking to one person at a time so you will feel less intimidated by a large audience and be able to develop a more natural delivery style.

- *Look long enough to complete a thought.* You don't want to stare. But you don't want your eye contact to be darting. Therefore, look at a person's whole face—not just the pupils—and look long enough to complete a thought or register a reaction.

- *Locate influential audience members.* When delivering a persuasive presentation, check the reactions of the decision makers and other people with influence. However, don't focus on these people to the extent that others may feel excluded.

- *Use your body as you make eye contact.* In a wide room, if you only move your head from one side to the other, the audience will begin to feel as if they are watching you watch a tennis match. To overcome this problem, turn more than just your neck and head when you look from side to side and connect with people sitting in the middle as you move your eye contact across the room.

- *Make adjustments for large audiences.* If you are speaking before a crowd of hundreds, try to find one person in each section of the audience to use as an anchor point for your eye contact. If you then start looking at people sitting around these anchors, you can be sure you aren't ignoring part of the audience. When lighting prevents you from seeing anyone, you still need to give the appearance of making eye contact throughout the room.

Facial expression: What the audience sees on your face will affect how they hear your message. Try to avoid the stony, deadpan expression of ineffective speakers. Instead, relax your face and use natural expressions that are appropriate for your message.

- *Use conversational facial expression.* Like gesturing, facial expression is very speaker specific. Use your natural expressions to connect with the audience.

- *Smile when appropriate.* Conversational facial expression does not mean you have to smile all the time. For example, you might want to smile when you introduce yourself, but avoid smiling out of nervousness or when discussing sad or serious topics.

- *Interact with the audience.* Try the technique of looking at someone in the audience with "appropriate" facial expression and mirror the look on that person's face. For example, if you want to remember to smile, look at a friendly face; that person's smile might help you express one of your own.

4. Vocal traits

Your voice should sound natural and interesting. To achieve this sound, avoid reading or memorizing. Reading causes most people to stumble over words and use unnatural vocal patterns. Memorizing leads to an artificial style because it usually sounds rehearsed. Instead, use a natural-sounding style. To do so, become aware of the elements that make up your vocal image, such as volume, rate, inflection, and enunciation. You'll want to vary the first three and enunciate in a way that suits the formality of the situation.

Volume: Your volume is determined by how loudly or softly you speak. You need to be loud enough for everyone to hear you, but you don't want to overwhelm people with sound. Many people can't accurately assess their volume so it's a good idea to go to the presentation room ahead of time with a friend; ask this person to stand in the back so you can test your volume. If you have a booming voice, you may want to lower the sound level a bit. If your volume is low, know that your voice will be even harder to hear once people fill the room. Since too little volume, rather than too much, tends to be an issue for many speakers, here are some tips to make sure you can be heard:

- *Speak to the back row.* If you have a soft, hard-to-hear voice, begin by speaking to the person farthest away from you and try not to let this volume drop.

- *Avoid vocal strain.* Learn how to increase volume without creating vocal strain. Begin by pretending that you are perched on a balcony, with the audience sitting below. When you attempt to send your voice downward, you will produce sound by pushing from your diaphragm rather than your throat. Your volume will increase, but you won't sound as if you are shouting. Even better, you won't strain your vocal cords.

- *Listen for volume drops.* Volume sometimes drops to inaudible levels in two situations: (1) *At the end of sentences:* If your voice trails off at the end of sentences, try pausing as you complete a thought; take in enough air to keep your volume strong all the way to the end of the sentence. (2) *As you introduce a new visual aid:* If people can't hear you when you put up a new slide, either talk to the people in the back row or pause if you need to turn away to put up a new visual.

- *Vary volume.* If you say some words or phrases with extra volume, you can emphasize them. For speakers with loud voices, sometimes lowering the sound level can also get attention.

- *Test the microphone.* If a microphone is creating volume for you, practice with it. You won't want to get too close or you'll hear a horrible screeching sound.

Rate: Your rate involves the speed of your delivery—how quickly or slowly you say your words and how and when you insert pauses.

- *Slow down if you talk too fast.* When some speakers feel anxious or excited, they tend to speak faster than usual. If you are one of these fast talkers, you will want to slow your pace when you are presenting. Try rehearsing your presentation at an artificially slow rate; as you present, you will recall this rehearsal rate and have an easier time slowing down.

- *Add pauses.* One of the best ways to slow your overall rate is to use more pauses. To do so, try to get comfortable with silence. Add an audible pause at the end of a sentence. Use this time to breathe deeply before speaking again. Pause briefly for commas. And try inserting a pause before and after an important message. It will make your point stand out.

- *Speed up if you talk too slowly.* If you speak at a very slow rate, try to speed up at times, for instance, when the material is simple. You might also try to vary other elements of your voice, such as inflection, to make your voice sound lively.

- *Adjust for cultural differences.* (1) Alter your rate so that it is appropriate for the culture. For example, in the Northeastern region of the United States, a fairly rapid rate is the norm; however, in the South, most people speak more slowly. (2) Consider your accent: if your accent isn't familiar to your audience, then slow down, especially at the beginning, so people can get used to your speech patterns. (3) Remember non-native speakers: slow down and make other adjustments as noted on page 10 to help listeners who are learning the language.

Inflection: We use the word "inflection" to refer to speaking with variation in your pitch.

- *Speak with expressiveness and enthusiasm,* in a warm, pleasant tone, with enough variety to create a lively and energetic delivery.

- *Avoid speaking in a monotone.* The opposite of effective inflection is a dull, robotic monotone that makes you sound as if you are bored. To improve a monotone voice, try saying long lists of words or numbers, using your voice to say some items with a high note and others with a low note. Once you've mastered making a list sound intriguing, you can then decide which messages in your presentation need the same sort of vocal emphasis.

- *Add low notes to a high-pitched voice.* Deep voices tend to be heard as more authoritative than higher-pitched ones. So, if you have a very high voice, you will want to learn how to lower your pitch and eliminate any shrill-sounding tones. To do so, practice diaphragmatic breathing as explained on page 139.

- *Avoid turning statements into questions.* When you make a statement, your voice goes down at the end of the sentence. When you ask a question, you use upward inflection. Some people unintentionally turn statements into questions, ending far too many sentences on a high note, which can make them sound unsure of themselves and decrease their credibility. To avoid this problem, practice driving inflection downward at the end of sentences.

Enunciation: Also known as "articulation," enunciation refers to how clearly you say your words. Whether you enunciate formally or informally should depend on the nature of your presentation.

- *To use formal enunciation,* you need to speak carefully, saying all your consonants and making sure your vowels are heard. Avoid dropping final letters (so that "talking" becomes "talkin") or squeezing words together (so that "going to" sounds like "gunna").

- *In less formal situations,* using such careful enunciation can make you sound stiff. While you do want to make sure your words can be understood, you don't need to use such precise articulation. In these cases, you can use contractions, replacing "do not" with "don't" and "you will" with "you'll" to create a breezier style.

- *To avoid stumbling over words,* in either formal or informal situations, identify the words that cause you trouble. For example, perhaps the word "similarly" is hard for you to say. If so, breathe before you use this word and think about each syllable as you say it. Sometimes you can rely on a synonym, perhaps using "likewise" to make your job easier.

Filler words and sounds: These verbal pauses are words and sounds that creep into your speech. Along with stutters, stumbles, and poor enunciation, they hurt the smoothness of your delivery. Some common fillers are "uh," "er," "um," and "you know." Using a few "ums" is natural for many speakers; if used only occasionally, they are not a problem. However, if used repeatedly, these words and sounds can become a distraction.

- *Add pauses to cut back on filler words and sounds.* If you overuse fillers, try to add pauses to replace some of them. Also attempt to become comfortable with silence; some people insert fillers because the lack of sound bothers them.

- *Listen for advanced filler words.* Some speakers have developed what communication expert Joann Baney calls "advanced filler words." These speakers create amazingly long compound, complex sentences by avoiding pauses and inserting words such as "and" or "so." They may also use needless phrases such as "to be honest . . ." (which may make them sound less than honest) or "as a matter of fact . . ." (which can be omitted and replaced with the fact).

5. Space and objects around you

Other nonverbal elements have to do with the space and objects around you. All of them will affect your delivery.

Space: Check out the size and shape of the room, its furnishings, and the distance between you and the audience.

- *Consider the seating arrangement.* Straight lines of chairs create a formal environment. On the other hand, a horseshoe or U-shape arrangement encourages participation and creates a less formal atmosphere. Even the shape of a table matters; for instance, presenting at a round table seems less formal than choosing to sit at the head of a long, rectangular one.
- *Factor in height and distance.* The higher you are in relationship to your audience, the more formal the atmosphere you establish nonverbally. Therefore, the most formal presentations might be delivered from a stage or platform. In a semiformal situation, you might stand while the audience sits. To make a situation even less formal, you might sit with your audience at a table or in a circle of chairs. Distance is also linked to formality. The farther you are away from the audience, the more formal you will appear.

Objects: Think also about the objects you choose to have around you, including what you wear.

- *Objects between you and the audience:* To increase formality, use objects (such as a podium or table) to separate yourself from your audience. To decrease formality, don't place objects between yourself and the audience.
- *Visual aids:* Interacting with your visual aids affects your delivery as detailed on pages 132–135. If used poorly, your visuals can become an unintended barrier between you and the audience
- *Dress:* Think about the audience's expectations and choose apparel that is right for the occasion, the organization, and the culture. For instance, what is appropriate to fashion editors may be totally unacceptable to investment bankers. Similarly, a suit that works great for an interview may look out of place on casual Friday. Avoid apparel that draws too much attention—such as exaggerated, dangling jewelry or loud, flashy ties. Dress to project the image you want to create, one that will enhance your credibility.

II. PRACTICE YOUR NONVERBAL DELIVERY.

You can enhance your delivery by using the rehearsal techniques covered in this section.

1. Check your content and timing.

Instead of reading from your slides or deck pages, prepare limited notes and rehearse out loud to become aware of content, timing, and nonverbal issues.

Using an outline for your speaking notes: Some presenters like to present from an outline. However, an outline used for speaking notes needs to be streamlined by

- *Writing phrases only:* Don't use complete sentences; instead print very short phrases for your main points and subpoints.

- *Using large lettering:* Make sure you can see your outline from arm's length. Leave lots of white space so it is easy to read.

- *Inserting delivery reminders:* You can add reminders, such as "speak slowly" or "show line chart now." These notes can help you remember what you are supposed to do as well as say.

- *Using note cards:* Most experts favor note cards over paper, suggesting that you put your revised presentation outline on 5" × 7" or 4" × 6" cards. You can handwrite these notes or print them from a computer, using a large font. Note cards have many advantages: they are easier to hold than paper if you want to move around as you present; they allow you to rearrange your materials easily; and their small size limits how much you can put on them. Typically, one note card should hold about five minute's worth of presentation reminders.

Making notes based on your visual aids: Other presenters prefer to print out copies of their visual aids and use these images as the basis of their notes. Sometimes they print their slides two per page and then add their speaking notes. If you use this technique, cut the paper into half sheets to avoid holding the floppy and unprofessional-looking large sheets. As another option, you might print your slides four per page, attaching each of the smaller images to a note card and including reminders below the images.

Rehearsing: Once you have your notes, you are ready to rehearse. If the material is complicated and new, you will likely need to run through it more than once, timing yourself to ensure that you won't run overtime. If your presentation is similar to one you have given many times before, you may only need to practice a few of the important elements, such as your opening, your closing, and the transitions you plan to use between sections.

- *Rehearse out loud.* In all cases, practice out loud. Knowing your content is not the same as saying it. So, don't just read over your notes, instead say the material out loud, using the vocal traits you want to use on the day of your talk.

- *Rehearse on your feet.* If you will be standing when you speak, then get on your feet when you rehearse.

- *Make adjustments.* An initial rehearsal will point out where your structure is weak, if you are missing transitions, and if you have too much material. In following rehearsals, you can focus on polishing your nonverbal skills and becoming comfortable with your visual aids (as described on pages 132–135).

Timing a rehearsal: Time control is important. Running overtime can annoy your audience and undercut your credibility. Only by practicing your entire presentation out loud, can you effectively check your timing. If you plan to use visual aids, rehearse with them to make sure you have time to introduce and show them all.

- *Time each section.* If you are rehearsing on your own, practice each section by itself and note how long it takes. Or better yet, record your rehearsal so you will be able to document the length of each section. As another option, ask someone to attend your rehearsal and time the various sections of your talk. With this information, you can make better choices about how to cut material.

- *Plan to finish early.* If your rehearsal reveals that you will end almost exactly on time, you still need to make cuts. Factor in the time you will need to respond to questions and the time the audience will need to understand your visual aids.

- *Decide how to make additional cuts.* Prepare to adjust timing further, if necessary, during your presentation. If you run short on time, do not rush through your points. Instead, plan to cut details and emphasize key messages.

2. Rehearse with your visuals.

Using visuals affects the timing of your presentation, but you also need to practice with them so you can gracefully integrate them into the flow of your talk.

Practicing with the equipment: Become comfortable with the equipment you have decided to use. Practicing is especially important with high-tech visuals and equipment you haven't used before. Don't lose credibility by fumbling with cords and searching in vain for the power switch. Instead, check out the equipment: set it up, turn it on, use the remote, insert and play the DVD, flip the pages, and so on.

Introducing each visual.   Even well-designed visuals don't speak for themselves; it's your job to help them communicate your message.

- *State your transition, then the main message.* To do so, segue from your current topic to the message you plan to show with your visual. For example, you might ask: "So what were sales results for the last quarter?" Then, pause before directing attention to the next visual, allowing your audience to see it, before saying, "Here you see that the Southwest office reached their $6 million goal."

- *Give the audience time.* Remember your audience has never seen your visual aid before; therefore, it will take them longer to grasp the meaning of your slide or deck page than it will take you.

- *Explain complex visuals.* When showing complex charts or diagrams, introduce the main idea and then explain the meaning of any symbols, colors, axes, or labels you have used. When possible, build complex images so you can provide this background information as you add various elements to the chart or diagram.

- *Cue the audience.* Don't assume people will know where they are supposed to look. Tell them. Show them. Or do both.

Controlling visual distractions.   Get rid of old visuals and glaring white screens. Also be careful not to let your visuals distract you.

- *Eliminate old news.* Once you are done with an image, remove it. You don't want to talk about a new idea while everyone is looking at an old visual. You also don't want a blank white screen behind you, so insert a plain black slide into your slide show or use the blank screen command on your remote (or the "B" key on your keyboard) to make the screen unobtrusive.

- *Talk to and look at the audience.* Visuals can become eye-contact magnets; don't let them disconnect you from your audience. For example, if you are writing on a board, don't write and talk at the same time. Otherwise, the audience will only see your back and might miss what you are trying to say. Similarly, don't look over your shoulder and talk to a screen. Practice until you will be able to focus your attention on your audience and not your visual aids.

Showing computer-generated slides: Computer-generated slide shows are among the most commonly used visual aids in corporate presentations. In addition to preparing a back-up handout to use in case of an emergency, remember these slide show tips:

- *Check the equipment.* Save your slide show on the computer's hard drive so it will run faster than if you use a memory drive or CD and practice with the cordless mouse. If using a laptop, turn off screen savers and the power-saving mode that will change your screen after a certain amount of time.

- *Check your slides.* Test the colors and animation to make sure your slides appear the way you intended. In most cases, the colors you see on your computer will not match those projected on the screen. Next, walk to the back of the room. Verify that all the lettering is easy to see and every slide is free of mistakes.

- *Practice introducing and building each visual.* Follow the tips on page 132 to integrate your slides into your talk. Go over all the cueing features you have inserted (such as the "build and dim" feature often used to add bullet points). Check the animation you have used to build complex charts or diagrams.

- *Insert extra slides at the end.* Either make extra copies of your final slide or insert several black slides at the end of your slide show to make sure an extra click on the remote won't send you out of slide show mode and back to the PowerPoint program. Endings are important, so guarantee that your closing message—and not the PowerPoint program—will have the spotlight.

Presenting with a deck: No matter how they are going to be used, decks need to be carefully proofread before they are printed. Check each copy to make sure the pages are in order and nothing has been left out. The following tips apply for times when a deck is your primary visual:

- *Preview with the table of contents.* Include a table of contents in your deck, and review it with the audience. For example, you might say, "As you can see in the table of contents, this deck has four sections. In the next hour, I'll (1) explain why the timing and environment are right for this new venture, (2) share some financial information that should interest you, (3) take you through our competitive analysis, and (4) introduce you to the other members of the management team who can turn this business plan into a profitable reality."

- *Explain how you plan to use the deck.* Let the audience know if you plan to go over all the pages or only a few. If you have included an appendix, tell them what's in it and how the material should be used.

- *Be flexible.* Deck presentations are supposed to be flexible and interactive. Be responsive to your audience by skipping a page that turns out to be unnecessary or jumping to a new section if appropriate.

- *Let listeners know where you are.* Help the audience follow along, by saying something, such as "As you'll see on page 12, most of our competition would be larger and far less flexible organizations . . . ."

- *Introduce each new page.* Begin by highlighting the main message, which should be conveniently located in your title. If necessary, explain your use of color and the elements of your charts or diagrams. For example, you might say, "Down the left side of the matrix, I have listed the five skills or traits we are looking for in an applicant . . ." or "The green bars on this chart show the base pay for each member of the sales team . . . ."

- *Don't read from the deck.* Talk to your audience and not the paper. If possible, place the deck on a table so you can gesture. Direct their attention to the deck pages only when necessary. At other times, make eye contact with the audience to keep their focus on you and not the visual aid. If a deck page has lots of print on it, do not read the text to your audience. Instead, give them time to read it for themselves or summarize it for them.

Using flipcharts: Use flipcharts to make your presentation interactive by recording people's comments or use them as prepared visuals for small informal groups.

- *Write so they can read it.* Choose thick markers in visible colors and have spare ones nearby. Include message titles if they will fit on the page. (If your writing is messy or you want to save time, prepare your titles ahead or have someone write them for you.)

- *Practice flipping pages.* Turning a page on a large flipchart can be difficult. Practice until you can do it with one motion. To make it easier to find a prepared page, bend the corner of the page on top of it. Label the upturned corner in pencil. When you're ready to show the prepared page, it will be easy to find because of the upturned corner.

- *Decide what to do with old news.* Once a page is no longer needed, flip it so the audience isn't distracted by an old list. On the other hand, if you want the audience to recall several pages, remove them from the pad and use tape to hang them somewhere in the room.

- *Remain focused on the audience.* Avoid writing and talking simultaneously. Instead, stop talking. Write on the flipchart. And stand to the side so the audience can see what you've written. When recording someone else's thoughts, try to look at the person as long as possible before breaking the connection to write on the flipchart. Check back when you're done to make sure you got it right.

III. MANAGE YOUR NERVOUS SYMPTOMS.

If speaking before a group makes you nervous, you are not alone. Surveys report that public speaking is the number one fear in the United States, more frightening than snakes, heights, loneliness, and even death. Nervous feelings are the result of adrenaline pumping through your body. Some common manifestations of speech anxiety include butterflies in the stomach, a pounding heart, sweaty palms, a dry mouth, memory loss, shaking limbs, a quivering voice, shortness of breath, and blushing.

The good news is that many of these nervous symptoms aren't visible or audible—which means presenters usually look and sound better than they feel. The audience can't see your pounding heart or sweaty palms. They aren't aware of your dry mouth. They probably won't even notice momentary memory loss. So take comfort in the fact that many of your symptoms can't be detected, and don't berate yourself for feeling nervous. Instead, try to regard the adrenaline rush as a positive element since your delivery might be flat without it. In addition, experiment with the suggestions described in this section until you find the one, or the combination, that helps you manage your nervous symptoms.

1. General techniques

Increase your confidence by analyzing your nervous symptoms and by reminding yourself that you are thoroughly prepared.

Analyze your nervous symptoms.   Identify what symptoms affect you and when they are likely to occur. For instance, you might feel better when you sit down than when you stand. Similarly, you might experience minimal anxiety when the material is familiar but start to panic if the topic is new. Or maybe the size of the group affects you. Some people prefer talking to small groups, while others actually feel more comfortable in front of large audiences.

Once you have thought about when your nervous symptoms are most likely to occur, group them as to whether they are visible or audible to the audience. You may want to focus only on those that are noticeable or you may prefer to begin with the symptoms that bother you the most.

- *Body language:* If your nervous symptoms are related to body language—such as pacing, fidgeting, or darting eye contact—review the material on body position, movement, hand and arm gesturing, eye contact, and facial expression at the beginning of this chapter (pages 120–125) and then try some of the physical relaxation techniques described later in this chapter on pages 138–139.

- *Vocal traits:* If your symptoms relate to vocal traits, review the material about volume, rate, inflection, and filler words on pages 125–128. Then look at the vocal advice on page 139.

Prepare and rehearse.   If you have followed the suggestions we have made so far, you have used an effective process to prepare and rehearse. This knowledge should build your confidence and help calm you down.

- *Be confident because you have used a strategic approach.* If you have "aimed," you have done the necessary strategic work. Your material will be appropriate for the audience, your objective will be clear, and you will have ordered the material so that it will hold the audience's attention and be easy to recall.

- *Benefit from having a clear structure.* If you have a good opening with a preview, then both you and the audience will be very aware of how you plan to structure your talk. If you have organized the body into a small number of sections, you will have no trouble remembering which section comes next. If you have created and rehearsed your backward/forward-looking transitions, you won't get stuck wondering how to move to the next part of your talk. And if you have prepared a strong closing, you won't use a dribble ending, such as muttering "well, that's it, so thanks" as you head for your chair.

- *Practice as suggested earlier in this chapter.* Prepare effective notes. You will have them if you need them. Rehearse out loud and on your feet since knowing something and saying it out loud are two entirely different matters. Check your timing so you don't have too much material and figure out what to cut if your presentation starts late. Make sure you know how to integrate your visual aids into the content of your talk and that you have practiced with the actual visuals you plan to use. If possible, do a rehearsal in the room so you can get used to the space and the furniture arrangement, too.

- *Get some feedback.* If possible, videotape a rehearsal so you can hear and see yourself from the audience's perspective. You might also invite someone to attend one of your rehearsals and ask this person to comment on your content and delivery style.

2. Physical techniques

The following set of techniques is based on the assumption, shared by many athletes and performers, that by relaxing yourself physically, you will calm yourself mentally. Experiment with some of these suggestions until you find one that helps you.

Exercise to control the adrenaline.   One way to channel all the nervous energy that sometimes accompanies a presentation is to exercise on the day of your talk. Many people calm down following the physical exertion of calisthenics, jogging, tennis, yoga, or another of their preferred athletic activities.

Try progressive relaxation.   Developed by psychologist Edmund Jacobson, progressive relaxation involves tensing and relaxing a series of muscle groups. To try this technique,

- *Set aside 20 minutes of undisturbed time* in a comfortable, darkened place where you can lie down.
- *Tense and relax each muscle group.* The various groups include hands, arms, forehead, neck and throat, upper back, lower back, chest, stomach, buttocks, thighs, calves, and feet. To tense a muscle group, clench vigorously for a full five to seven seconds. To relax, release the tension very quickly. You should experience a warm and pleasant sensation after relaxing each muscle group.
- *Repeat the process.* Tense and relax each muscle group, one after the other. Do the entire process at least twice.

Relax specific body parts.   For some people, stage fright manifests itself in certain parts of the body—for example, tense shoulders, quivering arms, or fidgety hands. Here are some exercises to relax specific body parts:

- *Relax your neck and throat.* Gently roll your neck from side to side, front to back, chin to chest, or all the way around.
- *Relax your shoulders.* Raise one or both shoulders as if you were shrugging. Then roll them back, then down, then forward. After a dozen or so repetitions, rotate in the opposite direction.
- *Relax your arms.* Shake out your arms, first only at the shoulders, then only at the elbow, finally letting your hands flop at the wrist.
- *Relax your hands.* Repeatedly clench and relax your fists. Start with an open hand and close each finger one by one to make a fist. Hold the position, then release.

Breathe deeply. Controlled breathing exercises are an effective way to lower your heart rate and calm down. The out-breath is the calming one; therefore, emphasize it and not the in-breath. Avoid breathing too fast or doing so much deep breathing that you hyperventilate. Try one or both of these techniques:

- *Emphatic out-breathing:* Breathe in normally through your nose. Then, breathe out through your mouth—with (1) an audible sigh; (2) a series of short, staccato bursts of air; or (3) one long, continuous stream of air, released as slowly as possible.

- *Metered breathing:* Using a count of four, breathe in and out slowly and comfortably—four in and four out, like a metronome. Then, keeping the same measured pace, breathe in to the count of four, hold the breath to the count of four, and breathe out to the count of eight.

Prepare your voice. Some nervous symptoms affect your voice, causing you to feel short of breath or to produce a cracking or quivering sound. Here are some suggestions for keeping your voice in shape:

- *Practice diaphragmatic breathing.* Diaphragmatic breathing reduces strain on your vocal cords, slows your heart rate, and lowers your pitch. But where exactly is your diaphragm? To find it, put your hand on each of the following places: (1) belly (hand over the navel), (2) high chest (hand over the breastbone), and (3) diaphragm (hand on the bottom half of your rib cage). Now that you know where it is, think of your diaphragm as a balloon. Inhale slowly to make the balloon expand. Inflate it fully to reach your sides and back. Release your breath slowly and the balloon should deflate. Practice inflating and deflating the balloon for at least a minute, preferably lying on your back.

- *Rest and wake up your voice.* Try to get enough sleep the night before your talk. Wake up well before your presentation time to provide a natural warm-up period for your voice.

- *Use warmth to soothe your vocal cords.* (1) Take a long, hot shower, allowing the steam to revive a tired or irritated set of vocal cords. (2) Drink warm liquids, such as herbal tea or water with lemon, which will soothe your throat. Although warm liquids with caffeine are fine for your voice, they can increase your heart rate. Avoid warm milk or hot chocolate because dairy products tend to coat your vocal cords, which can cause problems when you present.

- *Do some vocal warm-ups.* Try humming. Begin slowly and quietly. Gradually add a full range of pitches. Then, practice making all the vowel sounds—"a, e, i, o, u"—and perhaps finish your warm-up by singing a favorite song.

3. Mental techniques

Some people find that mental relaxation techniques work better for them—that mental relaxation causes physical relaxation.

Try a positive approach.   Base your thinking on Dale Carnegie's argument: "To feel brave, act as if you are brave. To feel confident, act as if you are confident." He suggests that if you "think positive," you can turn your adrenaline rush into positive energy, motivating the butterflies you feel in your stomach to fly in formation and transforming your negative energy into a positive force. To try this approach, act confident and repeat positive words or phrases before you present, such as "poised, positive, and prepared, poised, positive, and prepared."

Assess your style objectively.   If you have seen and heard a recording of yourself, you should be able to describe, rather than judge, your behaviors. Instead of saying "I looked pathetic in that fig leaf position," notice that your hands were clasped in front of you during the opening of your rehearsal. Then, change your thinking, either by refining your delivery behaviors or by accepting them as part of your style. To stay away from judgmental thinking, try one of the following approaches (1) think rationally, as described next, or (2) create a positive self-image, as explained on the following page.

Think rationally.   Escape the "ABCs of emotional reactions" as described by psychologist Albert Ellis. Move beyond the ABCs to reach D, where you are able to dispute the emotional trap:

   A: **A**ctivating event (such as a nervous gesture or distracting movement) sparks an irrational . . .

   B: **B**elief system (such as "What a disaster" or "If I don't look perfect, then I'm terrible"), which causes . . .

   C: **C**onsequences (such as speech anxiety or depression) that can be transcended by . . .

   D: **D**isputing the irrational belief system with rational thought (such as "Now that I'm aware of this gesture, I can work to gradually eliminate it" or "I don't demand perfection from other speakers so why do I demand it from myself?").

Create a positive self-image.   Some speakers find positive self-pictures work better than motivational words.

- *Visualize yourself as a successful speaker.* Act out the visualization in your head; see the movie of your upcoming talk, including your polished delivery behaviors and the favorable expressions on the faces in the audience. You may even want to hear their applause.
- *Look at a positive image.* Replay a recording of yourself giving a presentation. Stop at the point where you really like the image, where your delivery style looks natural and confident. Remember this image when it's time for your next presentation.
- *Imagine yourself as the guru.* To remind yourself that you know your subject matter, remember the times that you have impressed others with your knowledge. See yourself answering people's questions and fascinating them with new ideas.

Picture a calm scene.   Relax by conjuring up a visual image of a pleasant scene. Learn how to take your mind from an everyday location to the relaxing place you have visualized.

- *Create a positive place.* On each of the several days before your presentation, close your eyes and imagine a beautiful, calm scene, such as the most beautiful beach you have ever visited. Add details to your image: see the various shades of blue, feel the temperature, and smell the air. Concentrate on your image, excluding everything else, and describe how you feel: "I feel warm and relaxed."
- *Juxtapose the stress.* Several days before your presentation, visualize the place where you are going to present. See the room and the audience; feel the stress. Then, distance yourself. Relax by visualizing the positive place you created for yourself.

Connect with the audience.   Think of your audience as individuals and not a vast group of unknown faces. Remember that they are real people, who probably want you to succeed.

- *Meet them and greet them.* When people arrive, say "hello" and talk to a few of them. These brief greetings may help you relax.
- *"Befriend" the audience.* Even if you can't greet people in the room, try to think of them as individuals. Imagine having conversations with them. You may even want to think of them as potential friends, picturing them in your home, enthusiastically talking with them in a warm and pleasant atmosphere.

4. Last-minute tips

When it's actually time to deliver the presentation, try a few of the following relaxation techniques. Some of these suggestions can even be used as you speak.

Manage your physical symptoms.   Obviously, you cannot start doing push-ups or practice humming when you are in the room waiting to present. Fortunately, there are a few subtle techniques you can use at the last minute to relax your body and help your voice:

- *Try isometric exercise.* These quick exercises can be used discretely to steady shaking hands or prevent tapping feet. Isometric exercises involve clenching and then quickly relaxing the muscles. For example, you might put your hands behind your back, tightly clench your fists, and then quickly relax your hands. Or, before you get up to speak, you might press or wiggle your feet against the floor, clench those muscles, and then relax your feet.
- *Take a deep breath.* Inhale slowly and deeply. Exhale completely. Imagine you are breathing in "the good" and out "the bad." A deep breath can slow your heart rate. Also use it to remind yourself that pausing gives you a chance to take in all the air your voice will need to make sound effectively.
- *Sip water.* If you suffer from a dry mouth, drink some water before you go up to present. Have a glass of water available as you present, so you can pause and take a sip, as needed.

Improve your mental state.   Also, at the last minute, you can dispel stage fright by using what psychologists call "internal dialogue," which means, of course, talking to yourself. Here are some of the messages you may want to generate:

- *Give yourself a pep talk.* Act like a coach and deliver motivational messages to yourself, such as "I'm prepared and ready to do a great job. My visual aids are first-rate. I can answer any question that comes my way."
- *Play up the audience's reception.* Look at the audience and find something positive to say about them, such as "These people are really going to be interested in what I have to say" or "They seem like a very friendly group."
- *Repeat positive phrases.* Develop an internal mantra that can help you overcome your fears, such as "I know my stuff; I know my stuff" or "I'm glad I'm here; I'm glad I'm here."

Relax as you speak.   Finally, here are four ways to relax while you are in front of your audience.

- *Speak to the interested listeners.* There are always a few kind souls in the audience who nod, smile, and react favorably. Especially early in the presentation, look at them and not at the people who are reading, staring out the window, or yawning. Seeing the engaged and friendly listeners will increase your confidence and soon you will feel able to look throughout the room.

- *Talk to someone in the back.* To make sure your voice sounds strong and confident, take a deep breath and talk to someone sitting in the back. Try to maintain this audible volume throughout your talk.

- *Know that you probably look and sound better than you feel.* Your nervousness is probably not as apparent to your audience as it is to you. Experiments show that even trained speech instructors do not see all the nervous symptoms speakers think they are exhibiting. Managers and students watching videotapes of their performances regularly say, "Hey, I look better than I thought I would!"

- *Concentrate on the here and now.* Focus on your ideas and your audience. Forget about past regrets and future uncertainties. You have already analyzed what to do—now just do it wholeheartedly.

In closing, we hope we have created an easy-to-follow guide that helps you prepare your presentation from start to finish. Whether you are an experienced presenter or just a beginner, we recommend that you:

- **AIM,** using the strategic framework described in Part I: analyze the audience, identify your intent, and make the most of the message.

- **Implement,** using the approach explained in Part II: structure the content, design the visuals, and refine your nonverbal delivery.

In addition to reading these chapters, use the index to find answers to your specific questions and refer to the bibliography to locate useful books, articles, and websites. And remember, you don't need to be perfect, but you do need to AIM.

BIBLIOGRAPHY

This bibliography serves both to acknowledge our sources and to provide readers with references for additional reading. On pages 144 and 145, it includes "classics" as well as more recent books and articles. It also lists several useful websites on page 146.

BOOKS AND ARTICLES

Adler, N., *International Dimensions of Organizational Behavior,* 5th ed. Australia: South-Western, 2007.

Aristotle, *The Art of Rhetoric.* New York: Penguin Books, 1991.

Baney, J., *Guide to Interpersonal Communication.* Upper Saddle River, NJ: Prentice Hall, 2003.

Bolton, R., *People Skills: How to Assert Yourself, Listen to Others, and Resolve Conflicts.* New York: Simon & Schuster, 1989.

Buzan, T. and B. Buzan, *The Mind Map Book.* London: Pearson Education, 2006.

Cialdini, R., *Influence: Science and Practice,* 5th ed. Boston: Allyn & Bacon, 2008.

____"Harnessing the Science of Persuasion," *Harvard Business Review,* October, 2001, 72–79.

Duarte, N., *Slide:ology: The Art and Science of Creating Great Presentations.* Sebastopal, CA: O'Reilly Media, 2008.

Evans, P. and M. Thomas, *Exploring the Elements of Design,* 2nd ed. Clifton Park, NY: Thomson, 2008.

Few, S., *Show Me the Numbers: Designing Tables and Graphs to Enlighten.* Oakland, CA: Analytics Press, 2004.

Flower, L., *Problem-Solving Strategies for Writing.* Fort Worth, TX: Harcourt Brace College Publishers, 2003.

French, J. and B. Raven, "The Bases of Social Power" in *Studies in Social Power,* D. Cartwright, (ed.). Ann Arbor: University of Michigan Press, 1959.

Graham, L., *Basics of Design: Layout and Typography for Beginners,* 3rd ed. Clifton Park, NY: Thomson, 2009.

Hall, E., *The Hidden Dimension.* New York: Anchor Books, 1992.

Heath, C. and D. Heath, *Made to Stick: Why Some Ideas Survive and Others Die.* New York: Ramdon House, 2007.

Hirsh, S. and J. Kummerow, *Introduction to Type in Organizations.* Palo Alto, CA: CPP, Inc., 1998.

Howell, J., *Tools for Facilitating Meetings.* Seattle: Integrity Publishing, 1995.

Knapp, M. and J. Hall, *Nonverbal Communication in Human Interaction,* 7th ed. Belmont, CA: Thomson Wadsworth, 2010.

Kosslyn, S., *Elements of Graph Design.* New York: W.H. Freeman and Company, 1994.

Linklater, K. and A. Slob, *Freeing the Natural Voice: Image and Art in the Practice of Voice and Language,* 2nd ed., New York: Drama Publishers, 2006.

Minto, B., *The Minto Pyramid Principle: Logic in Writing and Thinking.* London: Minto International, Inc., 2007.

Munter, M., "Cross-Cultural Communication for Managers," *Business Horizons,* May/June, 1993.

_____ *Guide to Managerial Communication: Effective Writing and Speaking,* 8th ed. Upper Saddle River, NJ: Prentice Hall, 2009.

_____ and M. Netzley, *Guide to Meetings.* Upper Saddle River, NJ: Prentice Hall, 2002.

_____ and D. Paradi, *Guide to PowerPoint.* Upper Saddle River, NJ: Prentice Hall, 2007.

Rabinowitz, T., *Exploring Typography.* Clifton Park, NY: Thomson/Delmar Learning, 2006.

Reynolds, S. and D. Valentine, *Guide to Cross-Cultural Communication,* 2nd ed. Upper Saddle River, NJ: Prentice Hall, 2010.

Schenkler, I. and T. Herrling, *Guide to Media Relations.* Upper Saddle River, NJ: Prentice Hall, 2004.

Sedden, T. and J. Waterhouse, *Graphic Design for Non-designers.* San Francisco: Chronicle Books, 2009.

Tannenbaum, R. and W. Schmidt, "How to Choose a Leadership Pattern," *Harvard Business Review,* March–April, 1958, 95–101.

Tufte, E., *The Cognitive Style of PowerPoint.* Cheshire, CT: Graphics Press, 2006.

Walkenbach, J., *Excel Charts.* Indianapolis, IN: Wiley Publishing, 2003.

White, J., *Color for Impact: How Color Can Get Your Message Across—or Get in the Way.* Berkeley, CA: Strathmoor Press, 1997.

Williams, R., *The Non-Designer's Design Book,* 3rd ed. Berkley, CA: Peachpit Press, 2008.

Yates, J., Persuasion: What the Research Tells Us. Cambridge, MA: Sloan School, Massachusetts Institute of Technology, 1992.

Zelazny, G., *Say It With Charts Complete Toolkit.* New York: McGraw-Hill, 2006.

_____ *Say It With Presentations, How to Design and Deliver Successful Business Presentations,* 2nd ed. New York: McGraw-Hill, 2006.

WEBSITES

www.berkeley.edu The Berkeley library system offers a comprehensive Internet tutorial to improve your research skills.

www.morguefiles.com Set up to encourage people to share and use free photographs, this site has links to a dozen other sites that also have free images available.

www.publicdomainsherpa.com This site explains copyright restrictions for using photographs and helps you understand what is meant by "the public domain." It also has useful links to many government image libraries.

www.sec.gov This site links to the plain language handbook provided by the Security and Exchange commission. You will also find a link at www.plainlanguage.gov.

Index